**Wallace-Homestead**

# Price Guide to
# AMERICAN

## *Country*

# ANTIQUES
## Sixth Edition

## Don and Carol Raycraft

**Photography**
Jon Balke
Carol Raycraft
Joseph Dziadul
Lee Sawyer
Laura Maupin
George S. Bolster
Michael Fletcher

Cover photograph by Jon Balke
Cover and Interior Design:  Geri Wolfe Boesen
Interior Layout:  Anthony Jacobson

Library of Congress Catalog
Card Number 86-640023

ISBN 0-87069-477-4

10  9  8  7  6  5  4  3  2

Copyright © 1986
Wallace-Homestead Book Company

Published by

Wallace-Homestead Book Company
580 Waters Edge
Lombard, Illinois 60148

One of the ABC PUBLISHING Companies

# Contents

# Acknowledgments

The following individuals contributed time, talent, or information to the development of this book.

William Grande

3 Behrs

Teri and Joe Dziadul

Cindy and Lee Sawyer

Ken and Carlene Elliott

Dr. Alex Hood

Opel and Joe Pickens

Richard Tucker

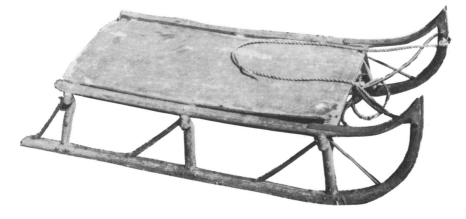

# Introduction

In the 1960s, "primitive" was commonly used to describe what has become known as "country." Primitives were usually kept in the back room, basement, or storage area of a neighborhood antiques shop that specialized in carnival glass, ironstone, and refinished oak furniture.

The primitives were acquired when an entire estate was purchased with the stipulation that the buyer take everything. The connotation of "primitive" was always negative to us. It was difficult to accept a skillfully crafted blanket box with dovetailed sides as a "primitive" when a factory-made table with a veneered top from the 1930s was called an "antique."

Primitive was eventually displaced by "country." Then, as the country look became popular in the late 1970s, we began to trip over country decorated plastic popcorn pails and birdhouses.

The current country mania is reminiscent of another period revival. After the Philadelphia Exposition of 1876, and well into the early 1900s, there was a "colonial" revival with a similar fervor in home decoration. The level of tastelessness of the period only recently has been superseded by the country can openers, lunch boxes, toilet seats, and macramé wall hangings.

In the 1940s and 1950s, the vast majority of the collectors of country antiques were interested in pine furniture that had been refinished. It is critical to understand that almost all country furniture made of "soft" woods (pine, poplar) was painted after it was made. The nineteenth-century dry sinks, cupboards, and pie safes that now are turning up at shows and in shops originally had as many as four or five coats of paint.

The growing appreciation and collector demand for painted furniture has created a unique situation. Many of the pieces that had lost their color forty years ago are emerging into the marketplace today freshly repainted. The price structure is such that a painted cupboard can be worth three to four times the price of a similar refinished example.

Unfortunately, as the cost of country antiques continues to climb, thousands of individuals who want the country look have been priced out of the market. Numerous country-oriented magazines, recognizing the situation, are not hesitating to feature homes furnished with a combination of country antiques and "contemporary" country.

We are now finding, in all sections of the nation, shows that specialize in "contemporary" country. The newly made baskets, stoneware, furniture, and decorating accessories range from serious investment quality to tole-painted metal wastebaskets.

The exceptional reproduction pieces that are being made today are going to create significant headaches for your grandchildren as they begin their collecting careers at some point in the future. It is going to be difficult to distinguish the "best" of today from the "best" of a century ago.

In the mid-1960s, a friend who had been collecting New England and Midwestern country antiques since the early 1940s commented that she was discouraged by the high prices she was having to pay. She lamented that escalating costs were going to destroy the interest in American antiques. We didn't understand her feelings because we had just entered the market and the prices we were paying were the only ones we knew. But now, after twenty years, a couple hundred thousand miles, a library of checkbooks, too many cold hot dogs, overpriced rooms at the inn, and only an occasional bargain, we find ourselves discouraged at paying $400 for something we should have purchased in the 1960s for $75. But while we are having trouble accepting the current price structure, new collectors are entering the market who will view today's prices as bargains twenty years from now.

# Suggested Reading List

Most local libraries do not have exceptional collections dealing with American antiques, and bookstores tend to stock more titles involving insulators, glassware, collector dolls, and fruit jars than on country furniture, stoneware, or baskets.

There are several major book sellers who distribute periodic catalogs of their offerings. All of them advertise in the *Maine Antiques Digest,* the *Ohio Antiques Review,* or the *Antique Trader.* The majority of the sellers who issue catalogs also have booths at selected antiques shows that offer hundreds of titles covering every topic of interest to collectors.

A library of antiques books at home is an invaluable research tool. A late-night caller from California once told us how she especially loved some of the color pictures in the first edition of our Shaker book. She indicated that a picture of a stack of painted oval boxes was invaluable to her when she was buying items for her collection over the telephone. The boxes served as a paint chart that could be used as reference for the approximate shade of a dry sink or a sugar bucket. She only had to count up or down the stack to get an idea of the shade of her potential purchase.

The ten titles listed below provide a basic antiques library for collectors. We have enjoyed each of the books and have learned a great deal from reading them.

**Advertising**
Clark, Hyla. *The Tin Can Book.* New York, N.Y.: New American Library, 1977.

**Baskets**
Teleki, Gloria. *Baskets of Rural America.* New York, N.Y.: E.P. Dutton, 1975.

**Folk Art**
Little, Nina Fletcher. *Little By Little.* New York, N.Y.: E.P. Dutton, 1984.

Simpson, Milt. *Windmill Weights.* Johnson and Simpson, 1985.

**Furniture**
Fales, Dean. *American Painted Furniture 1660–1880.* New York, N.Y.: E.P. Dutton, 1972.

Kirk, John. *The Impecunious Collector's Guide to American Antiques.* New York, N.Y.: Alfred Knopf, 1975.

Voss, Thomas. *Antique American Country Furniture, A Field Guide.* Philadelphia, Pa: J.P. Lippincott Company, 1978.

**Lighting**
*Early Lighting. A Pictorial Guide.* Wethersfield, Conn.: The Rushlight Club, 1972.

**Stoneware**
Osgood, Cornelius. *The Jug and Related Stoneware of Bennington.* Rutland, Vt.: Charles E. Tuttle & Company, 1971.

**Woodenware**
Gould, Mary Earle. *Early American Woodenware.* Rutland, Vt.: Charles E. Tuttle, 1962.

# Restaurant Guide

In several previous editions of this book we have provided lists of restaurants that were essential stops for us in our travels.

Texas attorney and antiques collector Richard Tucker has provided us with his semi-definitive guide.

## The Village Inn
Minier, Illinois
309-392-2327
A "must" for dining in the center of the state of Illinois. Enormous portions of steaks, chops, fried chicken, and the like. Excellent salad bar, and a variety of homemade breads.

## Paris Coffee Shop
700 West Magnolia Avenue
Fort Worth, Texas
817-335-2041
A local institution, where bluebloods and blue collars congregate for the country-size portions of eggs, Eckrich sausage, grits, meatloaf, chicken livers, and homemade biscuits and desserts. Open Monday through Saturday for breakfast and lunch only. Closed Sunday.

## Rancho de Chimayo
Route 529 off of Route 76
Chimayo, New Mexico
505-351-4444
Owned by a New York architect and housed in family's adobe just north of Santa Fe. Charming atmosphere and traditional New Mexico-style Mexican food. Dinner served on luminaria-lighted patio when the weather permits. Open Tuesday through Sunday, noon to 9 p.m. Closed in January.

## Pascal Manale's
1838 Napoleon Avenue
New Orleans, Louisiana
504-895-4877
Well-known watering hole frequented by sports figures and local celebrities. Justly famous for barbecued shrimp (free bibs provided). The pan roast is also recommended. Open 11:45 a.m. to 10 p.m., Monday through Friday; 4 p.m. to 10:30 p.m., Saturday; 4 p.m. to 10 p.m., Sunday.

## Durgin Park
30 North Market Street
Boston, Massachusetts
617-227-2038
If noise, less-than-genteel waitresses, and sharing tables with absolute strangers doesn't bother you, treat yourself to a New England meal at this Boston institution. Located in historic Faneuil Hall at Quincy Market. Open daily for lunch and dinner.

## Sally's Apizza
237 Wooster Street
New Haven, Connecticut
203-524-5271
Simply the best pizza in North America. The razor-thin, free-form crust pies are baked in brick ovens. Try the unique clam pie. Always mobbed by Yalies and other pizza aficionados. If closed or too crowded, try Pepe's just down the street.

## Mount Cube Farm

Route 25A between Orford and Wentworth, New Hampshire
603-353-4814

Former New Hampshire Governor and Mrs. Meldrim Thompson serve breakfast at their three-table shop located on their farm. The cornmeal pancakes (Mrs. Thompson's secret recipe) are doused with syrup from their maple trees. Mail-order gift boxes of pancake mix, syrup, and jellies are also available. Open for breakfast only.

## Tadich Grill

240 California Street
San Francisco, California
415-391-2373

A quintessential seafood restaurant located in San Francisco's financial district. You may have to belly up to the U-shaped bar in the middle of the restaurant while you wait for a table, but it's worth waiting for the impeccably fresh charcoal-broiled seafood. Massive menu. Open Monday through Saturday, 11:30 a.m. to 8:15 p.m. Closed Sunday.

## Also Recommended

Angelo's (barbecue), Fort Worth, Texas
Sweet's (seafood), New York City, New York
Louie Mueller's (barbecue), Taylor, Texas
McGehee's Catfish Farm (home-grown catfish), Marietta, Oklahoma
Kincaid's (hamburgers), Fort Worth, Texas
Carnegie Deli (delicatessen), New York City, New York

# 1 Country Furniture

**Pine dry sink-cupboard**
Red painted finish, c. mid nineteenth century.

**$1,200-1,500**

W hen you collect country furniture, you must have some basic knowledge before you load your four-figure purchases into the back of your station wagon. At today's prices, a "mistake" can be more difficult to unload than your brother-in-law and his mother on Thanksgiving.

As the market for painted furniture grows, many pieces that were flawed and refinished are receiving a second life by being repainted. The new "old" paint can cover a multitude of structural repairs and increase a piece's value.

**Arrow-back side chair** Painted finish, c. late nine-teenth century. **$75-100**

In the past few years, we have attended shows and outdoor markets from Maine to Texas. At each event we have seen numerous examples of pine furniture with painted finishes enhanced, restored, or completely re-done. Many of the cupboards, dry sinks, tables, and pie safes appear to have been painted with a broom dipped into a vat of Rustoleum. Some selected pieces have been more skill-fully painted and are sold quickly.

In 1985, we attended a heavily promoted show in Texas that empha-sized country antiques. A friend asked us to examine a cupboard that had been pulled from the floor of the show by the manager. From a dis-tance, the cupboard appeared to be a spectacular piece in great blue paint, but closer examination suggested that its paint was only slightly older than the pizza we had eaten the night before. We moved the cupboard sev-eral feet to get a better look at it and immediately noticed how "tight" it was. Normally the boards on a piece of furniture shrink with age, and nails slowly begin to work free. This provides the piece with some flexibil-ity. The boards on the back gradually separate and pull apart because wood shrinks across the grain. But the boards on this blue cupboard were as flush as the day they had been nailed into place. We had to agree with the manager—this piece certainly wasn't very old.

If a collector approaches a piece of furniture with an objective view-point that limits the level of emo-tional involvement, the chances of being victimized are significantly decreased.

The information that follows is designed to assist you in your search.

**Pine open cupboard**
Painted, c. mid nineteenth century.

## Notes on Collecting Country Furniture

- An "old" piece of furniture must show evidence of use. The legs of a chair or table should show that they were kicked periodically, and the paint should probably be chipped. Table tops were scrubbed down after meals, and paint was gradually worn away. The finish around drawer knobs was subject to damage and wear over time. The pine cup-board illustrates this point. It was opened by pulling the knob and also by grabbing a side of the door.

- A cupboard can be described as a "blind front," "glazed front," or "open." A blind cupboard has doors and no glass or "lights." A glazed cupboard contains doors with individual panes of glass. An open cupboard has no upper doors or glass.

  A cupboard that loses its doors often becomes more valuable as an "open" cupboard. Be on the lookout for hinge holes, excessive wear where the door would have been open and closed, and new paint added to match areas that had not been previously exposed.

  This open cupboard is a stepback with the upper portion of the piece recessed about 5″ from the bottom. Many stepback cupboards were constructed in two parts. A "marriage" of an upper case with the lower case of a second cupboard that has also lost its mate has been known to occur. The backboards on both sections of genuine two-piece cupboards should match in color, construction technique, and in the width of the boards.

- Most six-board blanket boxes are made of pine and painted. The sides are usually butted together and nailed. The box pictured has dovetailed sides and "breadboard" ends to control shrinkage. Blanket boxes can be found with replaced tops. It is important to notice if there are any extra hinge holes on the box that do not match with the holes on the inside of the top. It is not uncommon for hinges to be moved or replaced over time. If the number of holes on the top and the box are not the same, the top is probably a replacement.

**Blanket box**
C. 1860–1870, pine, painted red.

13

- There is an extensive variety of country side chairs available to collectors. Most of the chairs made by country craftsmen during the nineteenth century measure 16″ to 18″ from the top of the seat to the floor. If a chair measures 13″ to 14″ from the floor to the top of the seat, it has probably been cut down. When height is added to the legs of a previously altered chair, it can be described as "pieced out." Chair rungs or stretchers within 1″ to 3″ of the floor may also indicate a cut-down chair.

- Most pieces of country furniture were made of pine or poplar and painted. Over a century's time, a piece may acquire three to six coats of paint of varying colors. The pine dry sink pictured is structurally sound and dates from about 1860. It cannot be used in its present condition, so a decision must be made about completely stripping the sink or taking it down coat by coat until a desirable color is found. The advantage of purchasing a piece of furniture in this condition is that there is absolutely no question about structural alterations.

- The strips of wood that hold the twelve "lights" or panes of glass in this step-back cupboard are called muntins. The muntins should line up perfectly with the shelves. When it is possible to see the edge of a shelf an inch or two above the muntin, the doors have probably been added or replaced.

**Pine dry sink**
C. 1860, probably Ohio or Pennsylvania in origin.

**Step-back cupboard**
C. 1840s, glazed front with twelve "lights," Pennsylvania.

**Walnut glazed front cupboard**
Probably Midwestern in origin, c. 1880.
**$1,800-2,200**

**Pine open cupboard**
Painted red, c. mid nineteenth century.

**$2,800-3,300**

**Blind front pine cupboard**
Raised panel doors, refinished.
**$1,100-1,300**

**Open pine cupboard**
Painted, step-back form.     **$1,500-1,750**

**Pine corner cupboard**
Painted, glazed front with twelve "lights,"
c. 1840.                     **$2,000-2,500**

**Painted step-back cupboard**
Blind front, c. 1860–1880. The battens that hold the doors together appear to have been replaced. There are shadows on both doors, indicating that battens next to the top shelf have been raised several inches. The center battens were removed so only "shadows" on both doors remain.
**$1,500-1,800**

**Unusual open cupboard**
"As found" condition, pine, c. 1875.
**$475-575**

**Pine cupboard**
"As found" condition, painted, c. 1900.
**$425-625**

17

**Unusual pine storage cupboard**
Turned legs, painted, paneled doors, c.
1850. **$700-800**

**Painted pine storage cupboard**
"Open" form, c. late nineteenth century.
This open cupboard appears to have had
doors. At some point, the cupboard lost its
doors and much of its value. A close
inspection will show a mouse hole that
has no reason for being where it is.
**$400-450**

**Painted pine corner cupboard**
Paneled doors, bracket base, c. 1840.
**$2,500-3,500**

**Blind front pine cupboard**
Step back made in two pieces, painted finish, c. 1850. Many country cupboards were made with separate upper and lower sections so they could be transported easily.
**$1,600-2,000**

**Storage cupboard**
Painted pine, worn finish, c. 1870–1880. The price of this piece would rise significantly if it were yellow or blue rather than a deep brown. **$600-675**

**Early pine storage cupboard**
"As found" condition, paneled doors, c.
1840–1850. The paint on this cupboard
is past the point of being worth saving. It
was exposed to the weather on a back
porch or stored in a damp basement.

**$300-400**

**Glazed front cupboard**
With a step back and original worn
painted finish, c. 1870.      **$700-800**

**Step-back pine cupboard**
One-piece construction, painted, paneled
doors, c. 1850.      **$1,600-2,000**

### Maple cupboard

Unpainted finish, paneled upper and lower doors, factory-made hardware, c. 1870. It is difficult to date a cupboard by its hardware. Most pieces of country furniture made after 1850 have factory-made hardware. Mass-produced hardware commonly was used to modernize or replace damaged hardware on cupboards or chests from the eighteenth and early nineteenth centuries. **$1,400-1,700**

### Late storage cupboard

Pine wainscoting, refinished, c. 1900.
**$275-350**

### Painted pine cupboard

Appears to have an upper shelf section that was a later addition. **$275-325**

**Open pine cupboard**
Painted finish, dish rails on upper two
shelves, c. 1830.          **$1,600-2,000**

**Storage cupboard**
Pine, painted finish, c. mid nineteenth
century.          **$750-950**

**Walnut cupboard**
Original unpainted finish, probably from
the Midwest, c. 1870.          **$475-550**

## Pine step-back cupboard

Glazed front and twelve "lights," two-piece construction, grained finish, c. 1840. False graining was used to change the appearance of pine or poplar. Careful brushing and paint gave the impression that the piece of furniture was made of mahogany, cherry, or some other more desirable wood.

**$2,800-3,200**

## Painted cupboard

Red stain, Shenandoah Valley of Virginia.

**$500-700**

**Kitchen storage cupboard**
Pine, paneled doors, c. 1880. There is a
wide variety of storage cupboards used in
country kitchens during the nineteenth
century. If this piece had pierced tins in
the doors or on the sides, it would be a pie
safe.                                    **$475-550**

**Refinished pine**
Jelly or storage cupboard, c. 1875.
                                        **$400-500**

**Storage cupboard**
Pine, painted finish, c. mid nineteenth century. The problem with this cupboard is that it has been partially refinished. The majority of the paint is still good, but it will probably have to come off to match the drawers.          **$550-625**

**Painted cupboard**
Paneled doors, New England, c. 1830.
**$900-1,400**

**Painted pine cupboard**
Probably Midwestern in origin, mid nineteenth century. Softwood cupboards of pine and poplar were made to be painted. Most original examples are found with three to six coats of paint. American softwood cupboards that were never painted are rare.                    **$1,200-1,400**

**Linen cupboard**
Pine, painted red, c. 1840, Pennsylvania.
                                **$1,800-2,400**

**Pine step-back cupboard**
Open front, c. 1840, painted finish. On occasion, due to contact with moisture, the base of a piece of furniture can rot to the point that it needs to be cut off and replaced. When that happens, the bottom set of hinges is often only an inch or two above the floor. **$1,800-2,200**

**Pine storage cupboard**
Painted finish, c. 1880, missing a piece of molding across the top. **$400-500**

**Open step-back cupboard**
Pine, painted, probably not as early as it
appears. **$575-675**

**Painted pine storage cupboard**
C. 1870. **$425-500**

**Refinished pine pie safe**
C. late nineteenth century. **$450-550**

**Poplar, factory-made pie safe**
C. late nineteenth century, "star" decoration in tins, painted. This is a fairly typical Midwestern pie safe from the 1870–1890 period. It has three additional pierced tins on each side. **$500-575**

**Pine and poplar pie safe**
Geometric designs in the tins, solid sides, painted red, c. late nineteenth century. If this same safe were painted in a strong blue, it would be worth a minimum of $1,100-1,500. **$600-750**

**Twelve-tin Midwestern pie safe**
Painted pine, c. 1875. **$600-750**

**Walnut pie safe**
"Star" pierced tins, c. 1860. **$475-550**

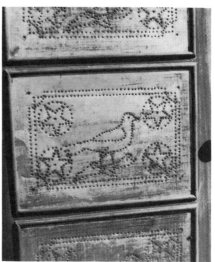

## Pie safe

"As found" condition, uncommon overlapping drawer on top, painted finish, c. 1870. When the tins are rusted through or damaged beyond simple repair, much of the value of the safe is destroyed. On rare occasions, a safe will be found with the family name, a date, or town pierced into the tins. **$250-350**

## Unusual poplar pie safe

Hand-punched "bird" tins, c. 1875. Factory-made pie safes often had tins that were machine-stamped rather than individually hand-pierced. Machine-stamped tins can be placed together and the holes will align perfectly. These tins were individually pierced and add much to the value of the pie safe. **$1,000-1,200**

**Painted pine pie safe**
C. late nineteenth century. Many late nineteenth-century pie safes have screen wire rather than pierced tins on their fronts or sides. **$400-500**

**Crudely framed pie safe**
Wire screening, c. early twentieth century. **$150-225**

**Compactly constructed pie safe**
Of pine, painted, c. mid nineteenth century. **$750-900**

**Pine pie safe**
Painted, unusually long legs, c. 1860. The purpose of the extended legs of the safe was to keep rodents from devouring its contents.

**Factory-made poplar pie safe**
Refinished, c. 1900.          **$350-425**

**Painted pie safe**
Pine, c. 1870.          **$600-700**

**Pine cupboard** $500-700

Above: Stoneware
cane stand
$1,700-2,300

Above right: Ele-
phant decorated
crock $7,000-8,000

Right: Storage
cupboard $600-750

**Step-back painted cupboard** $1,500-2,000

**Painted butter churn**
**$125-140**

Left: Collection of granite ware
$25-75 each

Below: Yellow cupboard     $750-950

**Blue high chair with new seat**                    **$385-485**

Left: Stoneware cooler  $3,000-3,400

Below: Low-post painted bed
$700-950

**Jam cupboard**       **$500-575**

**Storage cupboard**       **$550-625**

**Blanket chest**       **$500-575**

## Factory-made kitchen cabinet
First quarter of the twentieth century, maple, original finish. These were made by the thousands in a variety of styles and were sold by Sears and Wards through their catalogs. **$500-600**

**Ash and oak kitchen cabinet**
Factory-made, c. 1920s, refinished.
**$550-625**

**Bedside table**
Turned legs, pine and maple, c. 1875.
**$200-275**

**Hired man's bed**
Found in Pennsylvania, pine with maple rails and legs, painted red, c. 1840.**$700-745**

**High post bed**
C. 1860, pine and maple.                    **$750-850**

**High post bed**
Pine and maple, painted red, c. 1860.

$600-700

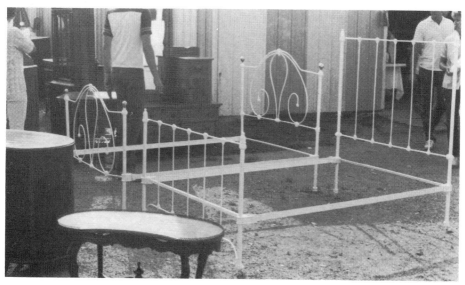

**Metal beds**
C. 1920.

$75-150 each

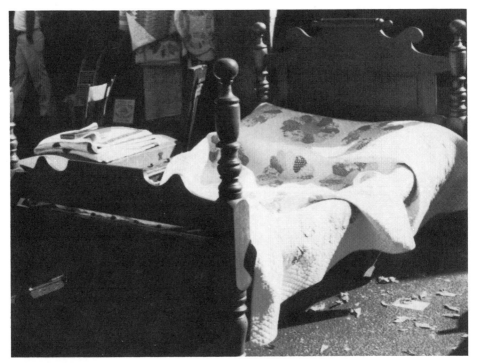

**High post bed**
Maple and pine, c. 1870.                                      $675-750

**Grained immigrant's trunk**
Scandinavian in origin, dated "1866," but probably from at least a decade earlier.
$675-750

**Hooded pine cradle**
New England, painted pine, c. 1840.
**$400-475**

**Stack of painted boxes**
Pine, c. mid nineteenth century.
**$150-350**

**Pine cradle**
Original unpainted finish, nailed sides, c.
late nineteenth century. **$250-275**

**Bracket base**
Six-board blanket box from New York
State. Painted, nailed sides. **$600-700**

**Pine cradle**
"As found" condition, c. 1880, nailed sides.
**$140-180**

**Decorated dower chest**
Pine, European in origin, c. 1830.
**$700-900**

45

**Dome-top trunk**
Sponge decorated, New England, c. 1820.
**$425-575**

**Six-board blanket box**
Painted and decorated, probably from
Pennsylvania, c. 1840.    **$800-1,100**

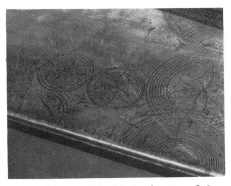

Decoration scratched into the top of the
six-board blanket box.

**Signed and dated storage trunk**
Painted pine. If the information on the
inside of the lid were painted on the front
of the trunk, its value would double
instantly.    **$400-550**

**Immigrant's trunk**
Dated "1836." Pine with heavy decoration, dome top. If the trunk is 150 years
old and the decoration is ten years old, it's
worth $450. If the decoration is original,
the trunk is worth $1,200.

**Painted, pine six-board blanket box**
C. mid nineteenth century. We literally
used to trip over painted blanket boxes for
$75 a decade ago. We haven't had the
opportunity to stumble at that price many
times in recent years.    **$275-325**

**Simply constructed pine table**
Tapered legs, painted, mid nineteenth century. $350-450

**Shaker table**
Pine and maple, red "wash" or light stain, New England, c. 1860. **$1,500-1,800**

**Pine table**
Painted finish, c. 1860.                                    **$700-875**

**Drop-leaf table**
Pine, painted, c. mid nineteenth century.
                                    **$700-850**

**Oak dining table**
Claw feet, c. 1880–1900.    **$1,100-1,300**

**Crude country table**
Pine, nailed together, c. 1900. **$200-240**

**Bedside or lamp tables**
Turned legs, c. 1870–1885.**$300-375 each**

**Sawbuck table**
Pine, painted finish, c. 1870–1900.
**$425-475**

**Pine table**
Painted, "scrubbed" top, c. mid nineteenth century. **$600-750**

**Firehouse Windsor chairs**
Factory made, oak and pine, c. 1900.
**$115-125 each**
**$700-750 set of four**

**Factory-made side chairs**
Maple and pine, c. early twentieth century. **$300-350 set of four**

**Factory-made dining chairs**
Maple with caned seats, c. 1900.
**$240-280 set of four**

**Windsor rocking chair**
Painted, c. 1830, comb on top of crest rail is possibly a replacement. **$500-600**

**Set of four factory-made side chairs**
Maple and pine, painted, c. 1900.

**$250-300 set of four**

**Set of factory-made kitchen chairs**
Originally had caned seats.

**$60-70 each**
**$320-360 set of four**

**Refinished maple wagon seat**
Splint seat, New England, c. 1850.

**$375-425**

**Country side chair**
Maple, painted red, replaced splint seat,
mid nineteenth century.     **$120-145**

**Ladder-back rocking chair**
Woolen taped seat, maple, c. mid
nineteenth century.     **$175-225**

**Painted settle bench**
Lift lid for storage, pine, c. 1830.

$800-1,200

**Rustic bench**
Caned back and seat, c. early twentieth century.

$200-250

### Shaker #7 rocking chair

Maple, made at Mt. Lebanon, New York. For a period of almost seventy years, the Shakers at Mt. Lebanon made rocking chairs in a variety of styles and eight sizes. It is extremely difficult to date a Shaker rocking chair accurately. **$1,000-1,200**

### Sack-back Windsor chair

Made completely of metal. Unique and difficult to date. **$600-775**

**Pine settle**
Storage area under seat, refinished, probably English in origin, c. mid nineteenth century. **$1,000-1,200**

**Arrow-back rocking chair**
Maple with pine seat, c. 1840–1860.
**$225-250**

**Oak church bench**
Refinished, c. 1900.
**$175-225**

**Pressed-back oak dining chairs**
Replaced seats, c. 1910.

**$175 each**
**$850 set of four**

**Set of four maple dining chairs**
Without seats and finish, c. 1900.

**set of four "as is" $240**
**set of four with a finish and replaced seats $400**

**Wicker rocking chair**
C. 1915, painted white.    **$200-250**

**Birdcage Windsor chair**
New England, c. 1820.    **$300-375**

**Loop-back Windsor side chair**
"H" stretchers, New England, c. 1820,
painted, made from several kinds of wood.
    **$900-1,200**

**Set of six Shaker chairs**
Maple, original splint seats, found in Ohio, c. mid nineteenth century.

**$3,600-4,000 set of six**

**Painted dry sink**
Pine, unusual base, probably Midwestern in origin, c. 1860.　　　**$900-1,100**

### "Skinned" dry sink
Pine, c. 1870. A piece of furniture that has been skinned or overly refinished normally loses much of its value.

**$300-425**

**Pine dry sink**
Refinished, c. 1870.          **$450-550**

**Refinished poplar dry sink**
Midwestern, c. 1870          **$325-425**

**Refinished pine dry sink**
Paneled doors, c. 1860.          **$450-525**

**Painted pine dry sink**
C. mid nineteenth century.          **$600-700**

**Pine dry sink**
"As found" condition, almost 6' long, needs a single board across front.

**$600-700**
**$1,200-1,500 restored**

**Pine dry sink**
"As found" condition, mid nineteenth century. **$375-450**

**Early pine dry sink**
Pennsylvania, c. 1840, painted finish. The classic dry sink consists of a bucket bench with doors added to the bottom sections.
**$550-675**

**Pine dry sink**
Made with commercially produced wainscoting, c. 1890–1910, original unpainted finish.
**$400-500**

**Pine dry sink**
From New York State, mid nineteenth century. **$550-675**

**Unusual pine dry sink**
Refinished, c. 1870. **$325-385**

**Pine bucket bench**
Painted, late nineteenth
century.                    **$375-500**

**Footstool**
Bootjack ends, painted and worn finish,
top mortised to sides, nineteenth century.
                                   **$65-75**

**Peddler's cart**
Early 1900s, stenciled lettering.
                                  **$350-400**

**Coffee bin**
Pine, stenciled "German Coffee," c. early
twentieth century.              **$300-375**

**Chopping block**
Sycamore, twentieth century.    **$200-225**

**Oak icebox**
Painted, factory made, early twentieth century. **$475-600**

**Factory-made spinning wheel**
C. 1860. **$300-375**

**Spinning wheel**
New England, mid nineteenth century.
**$200-275**

**Farrier or horseshoer's box**
Pine, painted red, c. 1880. **$125-150**

**Factory-made chest of drawers**
Painted poplar, c. 1900. **$275-325**

**Oak commode**
Factory made, replaced hardware, refinished, first quarter of the twentieth century. **$200-285**

**Flax wheel**
C. 1840. **$150-200**

**Painted pine storage chest**
New porcelain knobs, c. 1870. **$200-235**

**Cobbler's bench**
Pine, c. late nineteenth century.                    **$500-600**

**Pine cabinet**
New false graining.                    **$200-250**

**Walnut chest of drawers**
Factory made, c. 1880.                **$385-485**

**Oak storage cabinet**
Cast-iron drawer pulls, factory made, c.
1890.                                 **$400-475**

**Three-drawer chest**
Early factory period, painted finish, c.
1850.                                 **$385-485**

**Stand for a pitcher and bowl**
Factory made, repainted, c. 1880.
**$200-240**

**Dentist's cabinet**
Oak, factory made, c. 1900. **$1,000-1,200**

**Apothecary chest from country store**
C. 1850, brush painted and stenciled.
**$10,000-12,000**

**Pair of walnut chests**
Factory made, 1880. **$475-550 each**

**Pine map or surveyor's chest**
Refinished, c. 1850. **$575-650**

**Walnut desk on frame**
C. 1870. **$300-375**

**Oak desk**
Original varnished finish, c. 1910.
**$250-375**

**Country lift lid desk**
Open bookcase, pine, painted finish, c. 1850. **$750-900**

**Maple and pine desk**
Painted, lift lid, turned legs, c. 1850.
**$500-700**

69

**Pine washbench**
Painted, early twentieth century.
**$95-130**

**Pine washbench**
Painted, early twentieth century.
**$95-130**

**Painted pine country desk**
Lift lid, c. 1880.     **$375-500**

**Pine washbench**
Bootjack ends, painted, c. 1900.
**$95-130**

**Spool desk**
Walnut, c. 1860.                    **$500-625**

# 2 Kitchen Antiques

**Candy containers**
Nodder, Father Christmas, c. 1890.     **$1,200-1,400**
Father Christmas candy container, c. 1890.     **$850-950**

In early America, there was quite an array of cooking and roasting utensils for the great fireplace. Kettles and roasters were standard equipment, along with rare utensils for specific purposes. Apples toasted slowly in a tin apple roaster while the sizzling juices were held by the curved shelves. Ale shoes, made of iron or copper, were thrust into the hot ashes to warm the ale.

At the table, wooden trenchers (plates) were used to hold meat, thick stews, or pie. Two courses were served simply by turning the used trenchers over.

**Apple roaster**
Tin. **$375-450**

*This chapter was prepared by Teri and Joe Dziadul and illustrates items from their extensive collection. Mrs. Dziadul offers a lengthy list of kitchen and hearth antiques to collectors and dealers. The current list can be obtained by sending $1 to 6 South George Washington Road, Enfield, Connecticut 06082.*

Wooden noggins also were used and passed from mouth to mouth. Made in sets consisting of graduated cup sizes, they were started on a lathe and finished by hand. Frequently there were eight sides, cut with a knife. Wooden sugar bowls also graced the table and came in graduated sizes. White sugar was available in cone form and was cut into small pieces with a special sugar cutting tool (a sugar nipper). What we call granulated sugar was obtained by crushing the pieces in a mortar with a pestle.

Milk was plentiful and commonly used. Buttermaking was a job shared by all the family. Milking was done by the menfolk, children skimmed off the cream, and mother or grandmother did the churning. After liquid was worked out of the butter, it was salted and shaped by molds or prints.

Itinerant workers came with their skills and wares and broke the monotony. The candlemaker brought his molds and candle dips, but used the wax and tallow of the farm. Milliners and cloak makers arrived to fit the womenfolk.

These events were an integral part of the early settlers' existence. Ruggedness, hardiness, and strength of character helped conquer the daily hardships, and the most was made of simply pleasures.

The most tangible evidence we have of the early kitchen is from surviving utensils and equipment. You will discover many objects hand-made by the village craftsman, or factory-produced pieces bearing manufacturer's marks. Kitchen and hearth an-

tiques are one of the most popular collecting categories, but beware of fakes and copies.

There are a number of fake butter molds and stamps in the marketplace. The seasoned collector can easily spot these fakes merely by form and color. The "carved" designs show no skill and lack total character. Kitchen utensils were made for use and will show signs of wear and cleaning.

Valuations throughout this chapter relate to the condition shown or described. Always look for the best possible example of whatever it is you are collecting and seek both quality and condition.

**Apple roasters**
Tin, handle in back provides stability by acting as third leg. Single shelf roaster is rare, c. 1850.          **$375-450 each**

**Spice chests and spice tower**
Wood, painted labels on drawers, c. 1870.     **$275**
**Spice tower**
Four-stack column of boxes that screw into each other, c. 1820.     **$295**

**Footwarmers**
Pierced tin, wooden frame, double hearts, c. 1850.     **$250-295**
Pierced tin with eagle design, c. 1859     **$595-650**

**Set of wooden noggins**
Finished by hand from a block of wood.
These pitchers commonly held cider and
were passed from mouth to mouth. C.
1820.     **$175-275 each**

**Winnowing sieve**
A harvesting tool for separating the grain from the chaff, c. 1820.  **$375-425**

**Spice box**
Compartmented interior, c. 1870.
**$225-275**

**Sugar bowl**
Turned on a lathe, c. mid nineteenth century.  **$325-350**

**Double footwarmer**
All wood, dovetailed construction, c. 1830.
**$450-495**

**Child's toy animals**
Horse, c. 1920.  **$450-550**
Steer with pull squeak, c. 1890. **$450-495**

**Fireplace broiler**
Iron, swivel brace to hold at an angle against the fire. Very rare, eighteenth century.  **$425-475**

**Lanterns**
Pierced tin lantern that gave little light, c. 1800.  **$295-325**
Copper candle lantern, c. 1840. **$375-425**

**Set of five sugar bowls**
Wooden turned bowls used to store maple or white sugar, c. mid nineteenth century.
**$325-795**

---

**Doris Stauble arrangements**
Old millinery materials arranged in old containers by Doris Stauble of Wiscasset, Maine.
**$125-195**

---

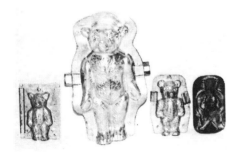

**Chocolate molds and cookie cutter**
Collection of Martha Dziadul Doak. Two-piece chocolate mold, c. 1920. **$325-375**
Two-piece large mold, c. 1900. **$150-175**
Teddy cookie cutter. **$85-95**

**Nantucket baskets**
Woven with rattan, wooden bottoms. Oval: Chamfered ribs, late nineteenth century.
Round: Single lacing around top, late nineteenth century.    **Oval $925-975**
**Round $625-675**

**Miniature baskets**
Handled basket, ash splint, c. 1880.    **$145-175**
Taconic, New York basket, c. 1890.    **$135-165**

**Milliners' heads**
Papier-mâché, usually French, used as working models to fashion bonnets, c. 1830–1900.
Left to right:             **$925-995**
                  **850-895**
                  **925-995**
                **950-1,050**

**Egg basket**
Wire basket for gathering eggs, c. 1875.        **$95-145**
**Egg rack**
C. 1920                  **$45-65**
**Pottery eggs**             **$10-12 each**

**Cranberry scoop**
Signed Makepeace, a Cape Cod maker.
Used to harvest cranberries in the bogs.
**$295-350**

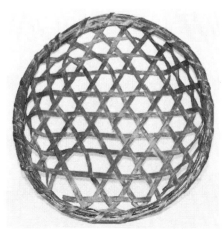

**Cheese basket**
Cheesecloth was placed in basket, and the
basket placed on a cheese ladder. Whey
drained from curds into crock or tub. C.
1860, poor condition. **$200-225**

**Stack of pillboxes**
Diameters 1¼" to 4". These tiny boxes
held pills or herbs. The smallest is signed
Julia H. Stevens and is dated 1879.
**$65-135**

**Framed candle mold**
Wooden box frame with twenty-four pew-
ter candle molds. Wires extend the length
of the boxtop to hold all the wicks. Mid
nineteenth century. **$1,100-1,200**

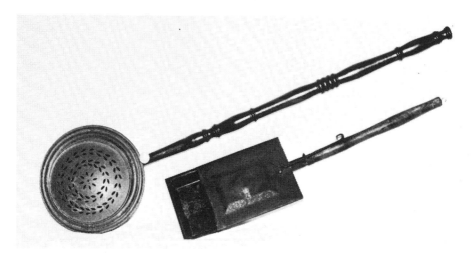

**Bed warmer**
Iron pan, filled with embers, slid between bed covers to remove chill. Circa 1850.
$225-275

**Fire carrier**
Early eighteenth century, cover slides instead of lifting. $325-375

**Chocolate molds**
Rare examples of Gaelic football, rugby, and soccer players. Marked Anton Reiche.
$225-250 each

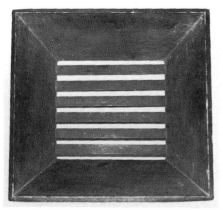

**Wooden cheese drainer**
To separate curds from whey after curdled mixture had been placed in cheesecloth. C. 1840, original red paint.      **$375-425**

**Tin pastry sheet**
A rare sheet of tin for rolling out pastry and cookies. Practical because dough would not stick and sheet never needed to be floured. A tin rolling pin should accompany this piece on the turned-up shelf. C. late nineteenth century.
    **$165-250 depending on condition**

**Butter stamps**
Two rare subjects—a horse and running fox. C. 1860.      **$850-950 each**

**Butter stamps**
Eagles. Handcarved, fine detail, c. 1850.
    **$400-450**
Simply carved, good detail, c. 1880.
    **$195-250**

**Butter stamps**
Hex designs. Early example of eighteenth century, deep carving.    **$475-525**
Outstanding eighteenth century geometric carving.    **$525-575**

**Butter stamps**
Eagles. Primitive carving with stars and arrows, c. 1820.    **$375-425**
Exquisitely carved eagle, rare example, c. 1810.    **$500-575**

**Butter stamps**
Double-sided tulip and geometric eighteenth-century tulip, carved tulip on back of knob
as well. **$675-775**
Eighteenth century geometric, primitive carving, classic example. **$525-550**

**Butter stamp**
Half-moon pineapple. **$375-425**
**Rectangular strawberry butter mold**
C. 1900 **$165-185**

**Miniature butter stamps**
C. mid nineteenth century.
Deer. **$625-695**
Lion. **$595-650**
Cow. **$195-250**
Grouse. **$350-395**

**Combination butter scoop and print**
Butter was worked into desired shape, then finished with the pattern on the print end, c. 1850. **$450-475**
**Lollipop butter stamp**
A very rare form and design, early 1800s.
**$650-675**

**Rectangular two-pound butter mold**
Unusual carved designs. Ear of corn, grapes, roses, clover, wheat, and pineapple, late nineteenth century. **$325-350**

**Butter stamps**
Miniature prints expressing rare sentiments. **$325-375 each**

**Butter stamps**
Pear and acorn and pear on branch, c. 1880. **$95-110**
Acorn and oak leaves, deeply carved, c. 1870. **$125-145**

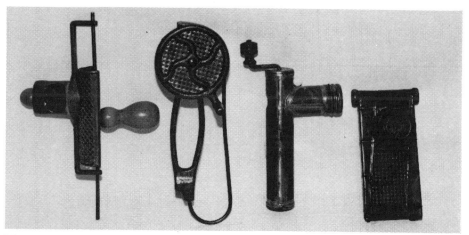

**Nutmeg graters**
The Edgar, tin, iron, "Pat. Aug. 13, '91."   $50-75
Wire handle.   $145-165
Massillon, Ohio.   $200-245
Tin, wood, c. 1890.   $110-145

**Crimping tools**
All-wood pie crimpers, carving on ends.   $75-85
Eighteenth century pie crimper and pastry marking tool, heavy brass and wood.   $225-275
All-wood pie crimper.   $95-110

**Pantry box**
Original sage green paint.   $125-175

**Biscuit stamps and prickers**
With iron prongs. All rare examples.
House in flames.   $350-375
Union with rose and thistle.   $225-250
Lamb and carved Innocence.   $475-575

**Chocolate molds**

| | |
|---|---|
| Bishop of Myra. | $95-125 |
| Pelsnickel. | $125-145 |
| St. Nicholas. | $125-145 |
| St. Nicholas on horse. | $145-165 |
| Pelsnickel. | $145-165 |

**Miniature tin salesman's samples**

| | |
|---|---|
| Biscuit oven. | $165-185 |
| Apple roaster. | $165-185 |

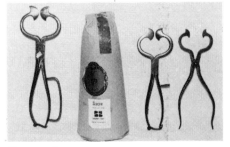

**Sugar nippers**
Used to break up sugar from cone for table use, mid nineteeth century. **$85-125**

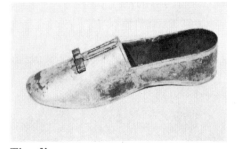

**Tin slipper**
Made for tenth anniversary presentation, c. 1920. **$225**

**Noah's Ark**
Wooden ark containing pairs of carved animals. Unusual, with iron wheels. In excellent condition.                                          **$1,200-1,500**

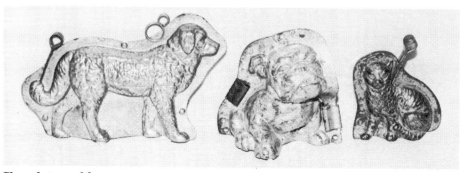

**Chocolate molds**
Large dog, Anton Reiche.                                               **$110-125**
Bulldog.                                                                **$85-95**
Cat.                                                                    **$95-110**

**Ale muller**
Tin, to warm ale.                    **$175-225**
**Ale shoe**
Copper, thrust into hot coals to warm ale,
c. 1840.                             **$295-325**

**Chocolate molds**
Rooster. $65-75
Hen on nest. $55-65
Rabbit on rooster. $85-95

**Miniature kitchen items**
Chopping knife, horn handle. $145-175
Saltbox. $95-125
Miniature wire basket. $75-85

**Candy containers**
Papier-mâché, c. 1920; ham, lobster, and turkey. $65-85

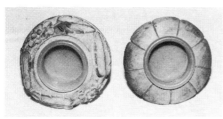

**Miniature salt dishes**
Deeply carved with Bristol blue liner.
**$110-125**
Simply carved with Bristol blue liner.
**$95-110**

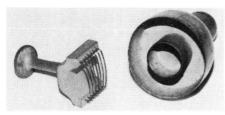

**Raisin seeder**      **$48-55**
**Doughnut cutter**
All wood, late nineteenth century.
**$75-85**

**Miniature granite ware pieces**
Basin.      **$25-35**
Bundt pan.      **$75-85**
Tart pan.      **$30-45**

**Preserve jar**      **$145-165**
**Pop bottle**      **$65-85**

**Cabbage slaw cutting boards**
Extremely rare carved cabbage rose
board, c. 1810.      **$275-295**
Heart cut-out hole for hanging board,
dated 1875.      **$225-250**

**Candle dipper**
Unusual square form.      **$185-225**
**Candle box**
Original blue paint.      **$165-185**

**Miniature granite ware pieces**
Roasting pan.                                           $35-40
Miniature pitcher with paper label.                    $75-85
Dish.                                                  $18-25
Ladle                                                  $35-45

**Wooden plates**
Wood should feel light in weight to be an early piece.  Eighteenth century. **$125-135**

**Blue Onion rolling pin and jar**
Marked Germany, c. 1900.
Rolling pin.                    **$250-275**
Very large Farina canister      **$250-295**

**Chocolate molds**
Running rabbit.      $55-65
Sitting rabbit.      $35-45
Rabbit bride.      $75-85

**Velvet rabbit**
Carrying velvet carrot. Note the slippers,
c. 1910.      **$425-450**

**Candy containers**
Father Christmas figures.
Papier-mâché, blue      **$425-475**
Papier-mâché, red.      **$425-450**

**Porringers**
Cast iron, T & C Clark, impressed Bellevue, c. 1829.              **$125-175 each**

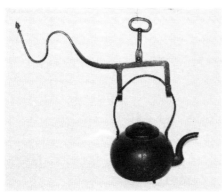

**Kettle tilter and iron pot**
Iron kettle tilter.              **$275-325**
Iron pot.              **$125-175**

**Redware fruit arrangement**
Plaster fruit in redware base, c. 1920.
              **$325-375**

**Carrier**
Original blue paint, four compartments.
              **$75-95**

**Candy tins**
Rare St. Nick tin with picturesque sleighs
on side, c. 1920.              **$85-95**
Three Bears cottage tin, c. 1930. **$65-85**

**Cake plates**
Sometimes used in three tiers, c. 1920.
**$38-45**

**Large cake plate**
C. 1910. **$50-55**

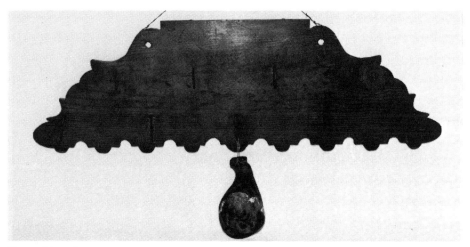

**Game board**
Wooden board with iron hooks for hanging game birds and small animals, c. 1870.
**$275-295**

**Tea caddies**
Boxwood apple form, with lock. Tea was a precious commodity in the eighteenth century and was kept under lock and key to prevent theft by servants. C. eighteenth century.
Apple form. **$795-895**
Pear form. **$625-695**

93

**Copper and brass cooking vessels**
Covered copper pot, dovetailed bottom, mid to late nineteenth century. **$145-165**
Brass kettle, multipurpose kitchen and hearth accessory. **$125-165**

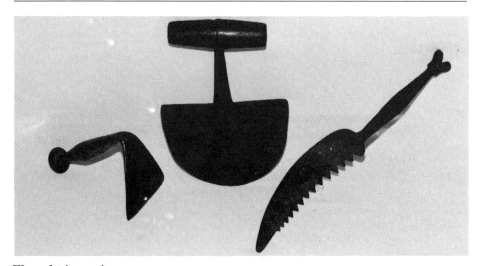

**Wrought iron pieces**
Dough scraper, Shaker origin. **$110-125**
Food chopper, expertly crafted by blacksmith. **$65-75**
Potato rake, very rare piece, to scoop potatoes from hot coals. **$150-175**

**Stone fruit**
Popular in Victorian period. Fig, pear, plum, apple, and banana. **$25-45 each**

**Bee skep**
Made of coiled rye straw, c. 1870.
**$145-165**

**Barrel butter churn**
Staved construction. **$85-110**

**Hog scraper candlesticks**
Early nineteenth century. **$110-165**

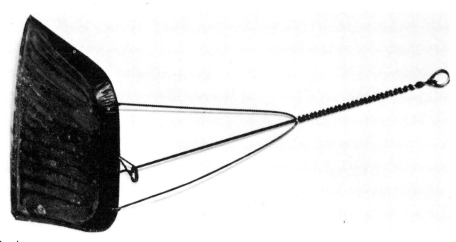

**Dustpan**
Tin with unusual collapsible feature. "The Never Stoop Dustpan, Pat. Dec. 6, 1898."
**$35-45**

# 3 Decorated Stoneware

**Two-gallon jug**
Whites Utica.  Slip-trailed Great Dane.          **$2,200-2,700**

When we first started buying stoneware in 1965, it was simple to find a stoneware jug decorated with a brush-painted cobalt bird for $25–40. Many antiques dealers paid little or no attention to stoneware churns, crocks, and jugs and sold them for a few dollars.

Over the past twenty years, antiques dealers have changed their attitudes. The most realistic prices for stoneware today will be found at shops that specialize in the field. Their proprietors are the most aware of current values, uncommon marks, unusual decoration, and skillful reproductions.

**Troy, New York, crock**
Floral decoration.
**$155-175**

General line dealers or individuals who only occasionally pick up stoneware often tend to overestimate the value of a piece and price it accordingly.

One of the nation's best collections of decorated stoneware is on permanent display at Museum Antiques and Arts, 153 Regents Street, Saratoga Springs, New York. Mr. William Grande has turned a 9,000-square-foot building into an antiques business with more than thirty dealers. Grande's collection is on display daily during business hours from 10 a.m. until 5 p.m. There is always an extensive array of decorated stoneware for sale to collectors. The Museum Antiques and Arts complex is closed only on Thanksgiving, Christmas, and New Year's Day.

The quality of decorated stoneware in the Grande collection is represented by the photographs that follow.

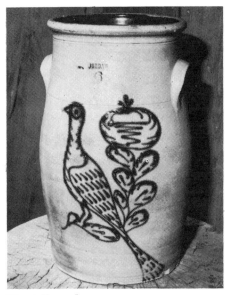

**Six-gallon churn**
Slip-decorated butter churn marked "Jordan." There is little question that the same hand used a slip cup to produce the birds on this churn and on the J.M. Burney crock. This bird also has the forty "dot" wing and tail feathers. The incised line that extends around the churn was added to give the potter a point of reference for applying the "handle" ears.
**$2,600-3,000**

**Three-gallon jug**
With impressed "Bergan and Foy" mark. Bergan and Foy was probably a store or business that ordered the piece. The jug appears to be a product of the Whites Pottery at Binghamton, New York. The slip-trailed bird with a spike tail stands on a leafy stem with blossoms. The "x" that is scratched or incised into the piece may indicate a reject or could simply be a counting mark to indicate the fifth or five hundredth piece produced. **$1,200-1,500**

**Whites Utica three-gallon jug**
The long-legged deer is standing next to a tall stump and under a rock cliff with a pine tree. The slip-trailed scene is strong on detail.          **$3,800-4,800**

**Five-gallon churn.**
Ottman Brothers and Company, Fort Edward, New York. The "velvet" antlers and flying ducks give this scene an early autumn perspective.          **$6,000-7,000**

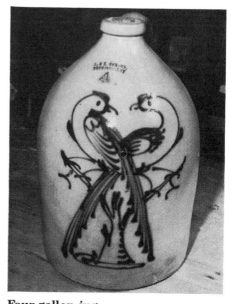

**Fort Edward, New York Pottery**
Four-gallon crock. The double "lovebird" pheasants have long droopy tails and are perched on a stump.          **$1,800-2,400**

**Four-gallon jug**
J. & E. Norton, Bennington, Vermont. Double "lovebird" pheasants.
          **$1,800-2,500**

**J.M. Burney and Sons**
Four-gallon crock. The boldly executed bird was created with a slip cup. The wing and tail feathers were made with forty elongated dots of deep cobalt slip.
**$2,300-2,800**

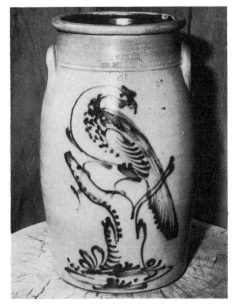

**Haxstun Ottman and Company**
Four-gallon churn. Elaborately decorated butter churns are extremely rare. This example from Fort Edward, New York, has an unusually large pheasant or peacock on an oversized stump. **$2,000-2,400**

**Four-gallon open-topped cooler**
Bennington Factory, c. 1820. This is the only known example of a cooler with the Bennington Factory mark. The cooler is decorated with a brushed tree and a splash of cobalt by each "ear." The "4" capacity mark was incised and then brushed with cobalt. **$2,800-3,500**

**Four-gallon open-top cooler**
N. White and Company, Binghamton, New York. Seldom will collectors find a stoneware cooler with an elevated base. This allowed a cup or glass to be filled from the spout, without having to extend the cooler over the edge of a table.
**$3,000-3,400**

**Three-gallon crock**
West Troy, New York. Incised running
elephant. **$7,000-8,000**

**Three-gallon jar**
F.A. Gale, Galesville, New York. The two
slip-trailed gamecocks are preparing to go
to war with each other. They take up most
of the surface area of the jar.
**$4,000-4,500**

The detail on this crock is so precise that
a small bird is perched on top of the stump
at right.

101

**Unmarked four-gallon crock**
Incised elephant. This unmarked crock was almost certainly made at West Troy. The elephant has an incised ear, tusk, eye, tail, and trunk and is running in the opposite direction of the other West Troy elephant. **$6,000-7,000**

**Three-gallon crock**
West Troy, New York. The bright blue cobalt horse tied to a stump is pawing at the vegetation under his hooves. Body was lightly incised, and the eye, nostril, and mane are more deeply incised. **$7,500-9,000**

**Two-gallon semi-ovoid crock**
A.O. Whittemore, Havana, New York. Slip-trailed trout. **$1,800-2,400**

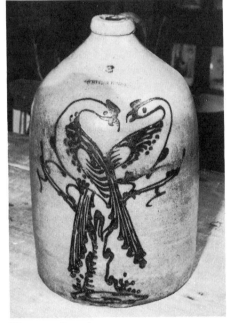

**Three-gallon jug**
Whites Utica. Double "lovebird" pheasants. **$2,000-2,600**

**One-gallon jug**
Cobalt scenes that depict human figures are rare. This example by Ottman Brothers, Fort Edward, New York, dates from the 1876 centennial and includes a man with a bottle of beer sitting on a keg. The length and condition of his nose would suggest that this is not his first bottle of beer. **$5,800-6,500**

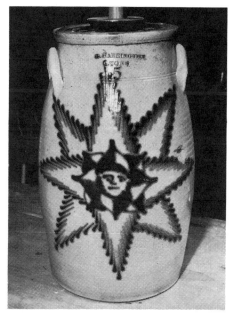

**Five-gallon churn**
T. Harrington, Lyons, New York. The eight-pointed starburst surrounds the face of a "jockey boy," complete with cap. It is fitting that this piece from the Grande collection is on display in Saratoga Springs—the site of the oldest continually operating racetrack in the United States. **$7,500-8,500**

**Five-gallon churn**
E. & L.P. Norton, Bennington, Vermont. The E. and L.P. Norton mark was in use longer than any other Bennington mark. It was used from 1861–1881.
**$1,500-1,800**

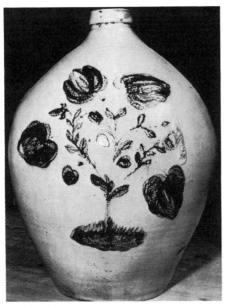

**Three-gallon ovoid jug**
L. Norton, Bennington, Vermont. Ocher (brown) decoration of a flowering tree or large plant. **$1,800-2,200**

**Two-gallon jug**
J & E. Norton. Large eagle or hawk perched in a dead tree and looking down at the ground. **$3,500-4,200**

**Whites Utica three-gallon churn**
**$1,200-1,500**

**Four-gallon crock**
C.W. Braun, Buffalo, New York. Turkey, with wing and feathers made up of more than 100 bright cobalt blue dots. **$2,800-3,400**

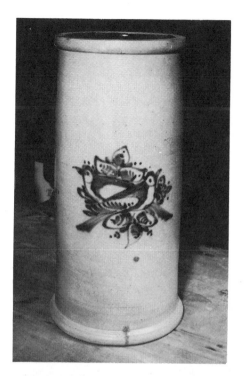

**Unmarked cane stand**
Three different cobalt decorations.
**$1,700-2,300**

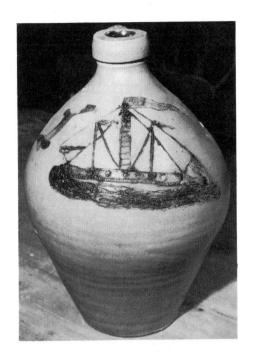

**One-gallon ovoid jug**
N. Clark and Company jug has five flags, masts, portholes, and a great deal of water filled with cobalt blue. Battleships, flags, and other patriotic scenes were made after major military confrontations or the periodic wars between 1800–1840. They are rarely found today. **$8,000-9,500**

**Five-gallon crock**
Haxstun, Ottman and Company. The body of the fourteen-point jumping buck is decorated with both lines and dots. Behind the deer are the remains of a large tree that has no leaves. Action pieces such as this jumping buck and the drinking man are much more in demand and command considerably higher prices than a standing deer or horse. **$6,500-7,500**

*The pictures that follow are from the extensive collection of the 3 Behrs. The 3 Behrs (RFD 8, Horsepound Road, Carmel, New York 10512) have been sending out illustrated catalogs of their stoneware for more than fifteen years. They have sold stoneware by mail order to collectors in all sections of the nation. The Behrs also offer an extensive list of stoneware-related books that can also be mail ordered.*

**Cooler**
Greensboro, Pennsylvania. **$800-1,200**

**Preserves jar**
Greensboro, Pennsylvania. **$200-250**

**Pitcher**
Molded, attributed to Utica, New York.
**$145-195**

**Lidded mug**
Attributed to Utica, New York.
**$125-150**

**Crock**
Standing elephant, signed W. Troy Pottery, c. 1880.            **$3,900-4,500**

**One-gallon jug**
Signed Yaeger, from Pennsylvania.
                                    **$225-255**

**Crock**
Signed Reidinger and Caire, Poughkeepsie, New York, c. 1870. The reclining deer is actualy a dog (whippet) with antlers added by the decorator. This is a rare and highly desirable piece of American stoneware.            **$3,500-4,200**

**Stoneware jar**
Fifteen-gallon capacity, stenciled decoration, late nineteenth century.    **$85-95**

**Moth design on ovoid jar**
Marked L. Norton and Son. Bennington, Vermont. **$750-850**

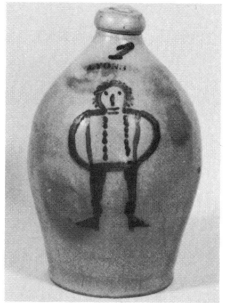

**One-gallon jug.** Signed Lyons, New York. Unusual decoration in cobalt with a man with his hands in his pockets.
**$4,000-4,500**

**Pennsylvania pitcher** **$675-875**

109

**Tree stump design**
Norton of Bennington, Vermont.
$700-800

**Pecking hen**
Norton of Bennington, Vermont.
$1,500-1,800

**Batter pail**
Cobalt decoration at spout and ears.
Unmarked.                    $170-220

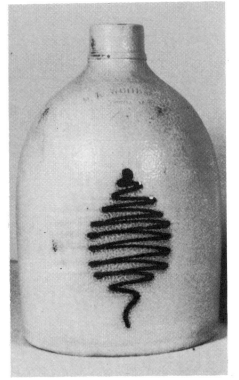

**Christmas or pine tree design**
Marked N.A. White, Utica, New York.
$150-175

**Pecking hen**
Unsigned, but probably made at Caire
Pottery, Poughkeepsie, New York.
**$475-575**

**Eagle silhouette**
Signed North Bay on two-gallon crock.
**$1,400-1,700**

**"Bird" jug**
Roberts, Binghamton.        **$600-700**

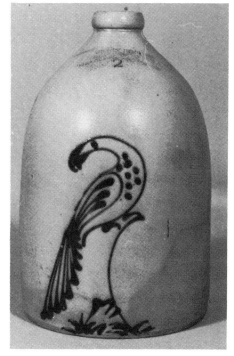

**"Flamingo" decoration on jug**
Whites, Utica, New York.        **$450-550**

111

**Reclining dog**
From the W. Troy Pottery, New York.
**$2,500-3,300**

**Ovoid jug, incised bird**
Marked Jacob Caire, Poughkeepsie, New York. **$1,800-2,200**

**"Bird" jar**
Whites, Utica, New York. **$425-475**

**Reidinger and Caire jug**
Double-blossom flower. **$165-175**

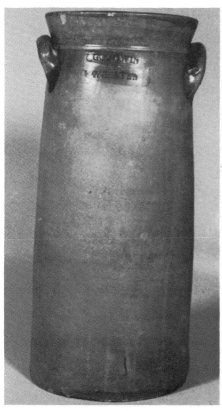

**"Cannon barrel" butter churn**
Marked Goodwin and Webster, Hartford,
Connecticut. **$200-250**

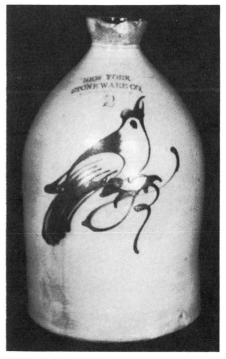

**Bird design on jug**
New York Stoneware Company, Fort
Edward, New York. The pouring spout on
the jug indicates that it was probably used
for storing molasses. **$375-425**

**"Dove" decoration**
F.B. Norton and Sons, Worcester, Massachusetts. Four-gallon crock.
**$500-550**

**Simple "bird" decoration**
Unsigned. **$275-300**

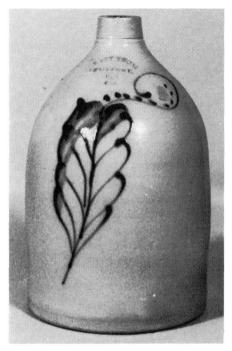

**Stoneware jug**
West Troy Pottery. Feather or quill
decoration. **$225-265**

**Pitcher**
Marked Burger Bros. and Co., Rochester,
New York. **$850-950**

**Dated jug**
"1872" from Burger and Lang, Rochester,
New York. **$275-325**

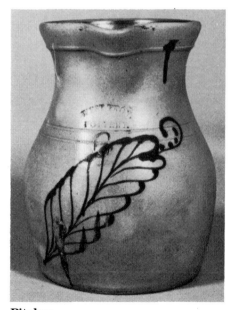

**Pitcher**
Feather or quill decoration, marked West
Troy Pottery. **$850-950**

**Crock dated "1867"**
Signed "Underwood."      **$275-350**

**T. Harrington crock**
Lyons, New York.      **$275-325**

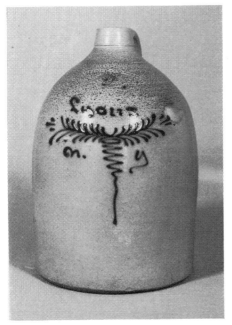

**Jug from Lyons, New York**
     **$165-185**

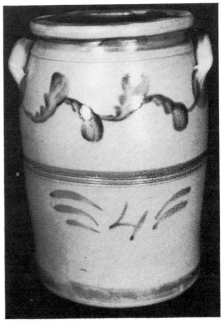

**Pennsylvania storage jar**
Unsigned.      **$275-350**

**Pennsylvania pitchers**
Unmarked, ½-gallon size.
$875-975 each

**E. and L.P. Norton**
C. 1856–1885, floral "bouquet" from Bennington, Vermont.
**$225-245**

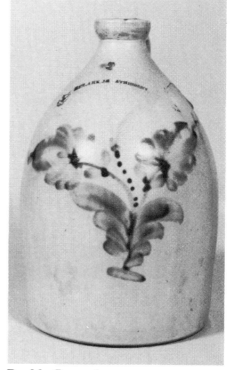

**Double flower jug**
Marked N. Clark, Jr., Athens, New York.
**$225-250**

**Advertising crock**
Unsigned, but probably made in Pennsylvania. **$185-225**

**Crock with floral design**
Sometimes called the "blue onion," Geddes, New York. **$155-175**

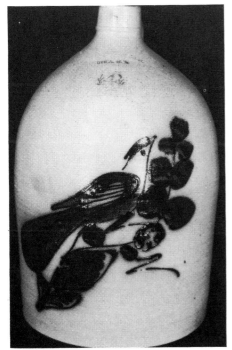

**Paddle tail bird on a hollyhock**
Marked N.A. White, Utica, New York.
**$675-750**

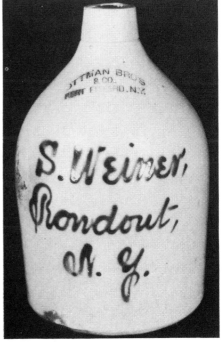

**Merchant's advertising jug**
Ottman Brothers, Fort Edward, New York.
**$145-165**

**Unsigned bird**
Banner on a stump.                    **$2,200-2,500**

**Jar with crossed American flags**
Harrisburg, Pennsylvania.  **$2,000-2,300**

**Running bird**
Whites, Utica, New York.        **$400-475**

**Basket of flowers**
Fort Edward, New York.        **$900-1,250**

**Dog with a basket**
Hart Pottery, Fulton, New York.
**$2,000-2,500**

**Unsigned shorebird**
Blue cobalt.                    **$450-500**

**One-gallon pitchers**
Decorated with birds.
**$1,500-2,000 each**

**Floral design**
Marked "Boone, Brooklyn." $275-325

**Ovoid jug**
Marked "Mead, Ohio." $225-250

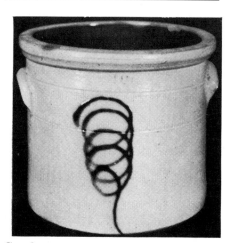

**Crock**
"Clock spring" design. $135-155

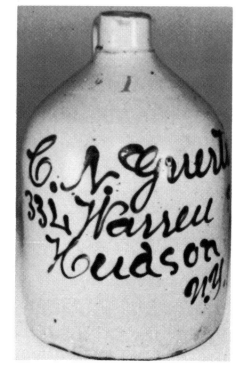

**Advertising or vendor's jug** $135-165

**Ornate molded, lidded stein**
Large stein (8½″ tall), attributed to Utica, New York Pottery.

$225-275

**Ornate molded stein**
From Utica, in smaller size (4½″ tall).

$175-225

**Match holder**
Probably made at Burger Pottery, Rochester, New York. **$120-150**

**Molded cheese jar**
"Nosegay Club Cheese." Attributed to Whites, Utica, New York. **$200-225**

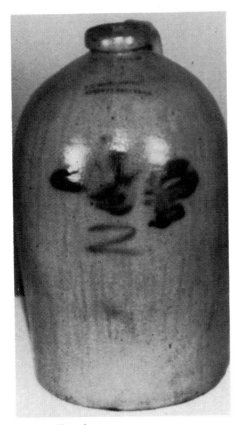

**Two-gallon jug**
Decorated with cobalt-brushed swirls, c. 1880. **$135-150**

**Bird and flower design**
Signed Farrar, Geddes, New York.
**$1,500-1,800**

**One-pint molded pitchers**
Attributed to Whites, Utica, New York
Pottery. **$135-175 each**

**Twin blossoms design**
Marked Mantell and Thomas, Penn Yan.
**$300-375**

**Lidded Pennsylvania storage crock**
Grape decoration on both sides.
**$725-800**

**Pennsylvania butter crock**
Marked D.P. Shenfelder, Reading,
Pennsylvania. **$350-400**

**Butter crock**
Greensboro, Pennsylvania. Stenciled
decoration. **$225-250**

**Unsigned butter crock**
Pennsylvania, with lid.  $400-475

**Stenciled butter crock**
Greensboro, Pennsylvania.  $300-375

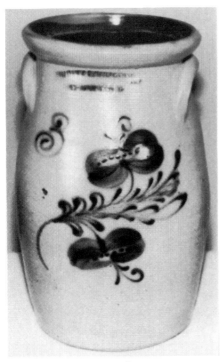

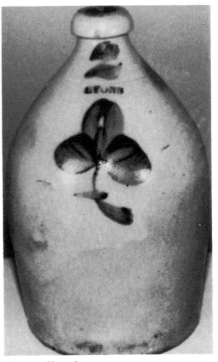

**Three-gallon butter churn**
Floral decoration, marked Hubbell and
Chesebro, Geddes, New York.
 $650-725

**Two-gallon jug**
Lyons, New York. Cobalt flower.
 $150-200

**Unsigned milk pan**
Probably from Pennsylvania or Maryland.
**$400-475**

**Triple tulip design**
Marked "Cortland," New York.
**$350-425**

**Jar with sailboat decoration**
From Cowden and Wilcox.
**$7,500-9,000**

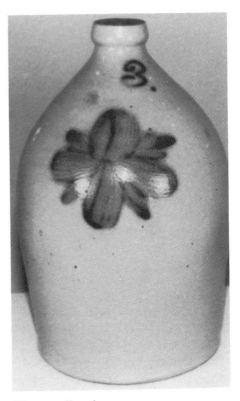

**Pitcher**
Stenciled decoration, from Greensboro, Pennsylvania. **$1,250-1,400**

**Three-gallon jug**
Signed Lyons, New York. Cobalt flower. **$200-235**

**Unmarked**
With bird decoration. **$335-375**

**Pipe bowl**
Unsigned, probably from Ohio. **$5-7**

**Jar with "bird in wheat" design**
Signed Miller, Newport, Pennsylvania.
**$1,400-1,500**

**Double bird**
Marked Ottman Brothers, Fort Edward,
New York. **$800-875**

**Molded mug**
Stippled design, attributed to Utica, New
York. **$75-100**

**Molded mug**
Also attributed to Utica, New York.
**$50-75**

**Milk bowl**
"Man in the moon" design, 1½-gallon, signed Cowden and Wilcox, Pennsylvania.
**$2,200-2,500**

**Flower crock**
Marked J. Burger, Jr., Rochester, New York. **$225-275**

**Floral design**
Stoneware jar, signed Brewer and Halm, Havana, New York. **$325-375**

**Twin bird decoration**
Unmarked crock.                    **$800-875**

**Batter pail**
Running bird, unsigned.        **$600-750**

**Hand-thrown mug**        **$100-125**

**Hand-thrown mug**        **$150-185**

**Stoneware jar**
Cowden and Wilcox "man in the moon" design.                    **$1,500-1,800**

**Stoneware jar**
With swan, signed Cowden and Wilcox.
                                    **$1,200-1,500**

**Unsigned jar**
Flower, stamped and incised ship (medallion) design.            **$2,500-3,000**

**Hen pecking corn**
Uncommonly large, unsigned crock.
**$450-550**

**Unsigned spotted bird**          **$335-375**

**Cobalt molded bottles**
Merchant's imprint.          **$125-135**

**Centennial miniature jug**
Dated "1876." **$125-150**

**Tall jar**
Signed C. Crolius, New York. **$900-1,200**

**Stenciled eagle on jar**
Signed Lion Pottery.                    **$850-950**

**One-gallon jar**
Brushed floral design.                    **$135-165**

# 4 Country Baskets

**Unusual storage basket**
Made with splint in twill or "over-two-under-two" weaving
pattern, c. early twentieth century.                **$125-140**

T he craze for country baskets has evolved in the past fifteen years. Even in the early 1970s, few people paid any attention to antique baskets, which, at the time, were priced from $15 to $30 depending on their form, condition, and original function. Cheese baskets were $75 to $100, and most of us couldn't conceive of their going any higher.

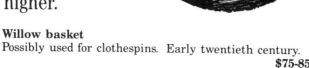

**Willow basket**
Possibly used for clothespins. Early twentieth century.
**$75-85**

In the 1970s, collectors realized that baskets had significant value and prices rose accordingly. Today the market for baskets is continuing to expand. Painted baskets are in great demand, as are uncommonly well-made or unusual forms. However, factory-made baskets or handcrafted examples with damage or major repair have not increased in desirability or price.

Future collectors are going to have to sort out the "old" baskets from the best of the reproductions that are now being made. The worst of today's reproductions aren't going to fool anybody and should not present too many problems.

Often the finest reproductions are almost as expensive as the original baskets. To further complicate matters, baskets can be aged prematurely by exposure to the weather. An excellent reproduction can appear to be a century old in a short period of time.

The pictures of baskets that follow are from the extensive collection of Lee and Cindy Sawyer of Virginia Beach, Virginia.

**Oak splint utility basket**
"X" bound wrapping on rim.     **$85-100**

**Melon-shaped utility basket**
Oak splint.     **$90-100**

**Melon-shaped utility basket**
Rib construction with blue weavers, thick hickory handle.     **$110-120**

**Oak-shaped utility basket**
Rectangular base with round opening, hickory handle, single-wrapped rim.
     **$115-125**

**Willow basket**
Used for holding bottles of wine. Early twentieth century, factory-made. **$60-70**

**Well-made oak utility basket**
Handle nailed to the rim. Early twentieth century. **$115-125**

**Oak splint utility basket**
Painted red, double-wrapped rim. **$200-220**

**Factory-made market basket**
Thick and wide splint, painted green.
**$85-95**

**Honeysuckle vine basket**
First quarter of the twentieth century.
**$60-70**

**White oak splint storage basket**
**$100-115**

**Tightly woven utility basket**
Carved handle. **$100-115**

**Crudely made apple basket**
Hung from tree by carved wooden hook
attached by a piece of leather. C. early
twentieth century. **$65-75**

**Oak splint market basket**
Unusually wide oak handle of thick splint. Baskets are rarely signed by the individual who made them. It is possible that their heavy use wore away any markings. On this basket, the name of the city in Virginia in which it was made is written in pencil on the handle. **$165-175**

**Swing- or drop-handled basket**
Red-dyed weavers, possibly Indian made, c. early twentieth century. **$75-85**

**American Indian-made baskets**
Similar to many sold to tourists between 1920–1940. **$55-70**

**Oak splint utility basket**
"X" wrapped rim, carved handle. **$110-125**

**Tightly woven ash splint basket**
Melon form, painted green, c. nineteenth century. **$125-135**

**Oak splint egg-gathering basket**
Rib construction, with wrapped rim, handle nailed to the rim, kidney or buttocks form. The buttocks form allowed the contents to be evenly distributed to both sides without falling through the center of the basket. **$125-135**

**Peanut-gathering basket**
From the eastern shore of Virginia. Factory-made, machine-cut thick and wide splint, painted white. **$55-65**

**Splint basket**
Intricately braided handle, used for carrying small logs or kindling, c. early twentieth century. **$110-125**

**Rectangular basket for storage**
Oak splint. The carved handles are carefully notched through the rim of the basket and held by the double wrapping and weavers. **$150-175**

**Dough-rising baskets**
Pennsylvania, made of rye straw, c. late nineteenth or early twentieth century. These baskets are built coil by coil and are bound by hickory splint that should have some obvious patina. **$100-125 each**

## Another newly made basket

Shows no signs of wear. Note that the notched handle has already slipped out of the grasp of the oak splint weavers that were designed to hold it. Like many new baskets, this example is not very tightly woven. Old baskets were supposed to hold things. New baskets are primarily decorative.

## Hexagon weave cheese basket

Wrapped rim, c. nineteenth century, 26″ diameter.                    **$650-750**

## Oak splint basket

Uncommon eliptical opening or mouth could have been used for pouring feed or grain. C. late nineteenth century.

**$200-225**

## Berry carrier

Also mass-produced berry baskets made from machine-cut, wide strips of softwood stapled together.

**Carrier and four baskets $20-25**

The rim of the basket is heavily wrapped with thinly cut hickory splint.

141

**Oak splint utility basket**
Carved handle, "X" bound rim. This is a fairly simple basket to make and is a form that is commonly reproduced. It is difficult to determine if it is five or seventy-five years old. Over time, basket handles acquire a patina similar to the knobs or drawer pulls on an old cupboard. Patina is difficult to fake and normally is obvious even to a casual observer. This basket is well-made, but not old. Basket buyers should look for signs of wear in any basket that was designed to be used.

**$75-85**

**Shaker-made feather basket**
Slide or attached lid, New England, nineteenth century.  **$325-375**

**Oak splint storage basket**
Carved handle, double-wrapped rim.
**$75-85**

142

**Collecting baskets**
A collector can spend years buying baskets one at a time. Sometimes the best prices and outstanding quality can be achieved by finding and purchasing a collection of baskets.

# 5 Country Store Antiques

**Coca-Cola dispenser**
Held ice water and bottles of soft drinks, c. 1930.

**$500-700**

T

he golden age of the American country store was between 1880 and 1940. Every community in the nation had a series of locally owned village or neighborhood stores that sold general merchandise and groceries and faced little competition from supermarkets. These stores were supplied with elaborately decorated patent medicine cabinets, seed boxes, coffee bins, and point-of-purchase counter displays that advertised their contents.

**Badger Roasted Coffee tin**                    **$40-45**

The "drummers" who traveled from village to village in horse-drawn carts or railroad cars also provided paper broadsides, tin signs, and samples of their wares to hand out to locals who congregated in the stores solving the problems of the day.

## Country Store Chronology

1809 Early techniques are developed for preserving food in glass bottles.

1830 Huntly and Palmer begin to pack their biscuits in tins for stagecoach passengers.

1856 Canned milk is sold in the United States for the first time.

1860 National brands become more popular than locally made goods.

1866 Bottled beer is available.

1880 Hundreds of companies offer a wide variety of chewing tobacco.

1885 Stores provide their customers with paper bags.

1890 Chewing tobacco is the most popular tobacco product.

1906 The Food and Drug Administration begins to closely monitor claims by drug manufacturers.

1910 Cigars replace chewing tobacco in popularity.

1920 Cigarettes replace cigars among the nation's smokers.

1937 Shopping carts and supermarkets gradually begin to appear.

## Notes on Collecting Country Store Antiques

• County store fixtures, boxes, containers, and display items can be found almost anywhere. But the odds of finding a #7 rocking chair by the Shakers at a house sale in Utah, or a Nantucket "lightship" basket at a Saturday night auction in Sarasota, Florida, are slim.

• It is just as possible to find an unusual store item at a show in Maine as it is in Iowa or Alabama. The golden age of the country store —the period when the most collectible store items were produced — was between 1880 and 1940. During that period there were thousands of grocery stores across America that had access to the advertising that is in significant demand today.

• Condition is absolutely essential in determining value. Unlike a piece of country furniture that can be repaired or refinished and still have worth, a store tin or display piece that has been repainted or restored loses most of its value. A tin container or bin that has been subjected to serious corrosion, scratches, or suffered fading by wear is normally not in great demand regardless of how rare it is.

• Paper cartons or signs with major tears, blemishes, or water stains have minimal value. Wooden boxes must also have their original paper labels intact.

• Prices on country store antiques have fluctuated in recent years. The degree of rarity of a particular tin could change overnight if several thousand similar containers were found in a warehouse in Des Moines.

On June 22, 1985, in Cornwall-On-Hudson, New York, a major collection of country stores items was sold at auction. The vast majority of the items in the auction were in pristine condition, and their selling prices reflected the demand for quality goods.

### Product tins
Peter Rabbit Peanut Butter pail, one-pound size, **$350**
Jack Spratt Peanut Butter pail, **$350**
Turkey Coffee tin, **$500**
Callanan's Breakfast Coffee tin, **$500**
Blanke's Mojay Coffee (woman on a horse), **$225**
White Bean Coffee tin, **$60**

### Cabinets
Humphrey's Veterinary Specifics with barnyard animals on tin, **$2,800**
Fruit of the Braider braid and spool cabinet, **$1,000**
Countertop four-door oak display cabinet on pedestal, **$425**
Bright Silk 25¢ Garter cabinet, **$400**

### Thermometers
Saucer's Flavoring Extract, **$525**
Lash's Bitters, **$300**

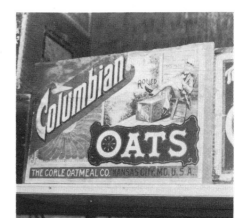

**Packing box**
The Columbian Oats packing box dates from the early 1900s. Most boxes are made of pine and are nailed together. The value of a box is largely determined by the quality and condition of the label. This label is colorful and contains a smiling Uncle Sam reading a newspaper. It also is in good condition.

**Seed box**
The Webster seed box with a perfect interior and worn exterior label is worth **$75-95**. If both labels were perfect, the box could be priced at **$150-175**. The box dates from the 1910–1925 period.

**Plywood sign**
The "Homade Hot Tamales" sign was purchased from a roadside tamale dealer near Argyle, Texas. The sign is of indeterminate age and has minimal value. If it were seventy-five years older and on a single piece of pine rather than plywood, we would be willing to stand in line for it. A survey of rural Texas school records indicates that the man who painted the sign was always the first to sit down in his fourth grade spelling bees.

**Store signs**
Country store signs have much more value than gas station signs from the 1950s. As the supply of store signs declines, the interest in other signs is going to increase. Signs of this type probably would be a good investment if you had somewhere to display or store them.

**Porcelain signs**
In recent years the porcelain notice signs that decorated doors in public buildings and restaurants have been reproduced in quantity. It is difficult to tell the old and the "old but never used" from reproductions. The Fairy Soap, Atlantic Coast Line, and Yankee Girl signs are reproductions.

**Chicago Cubs Chewing Tobacco**
C. 1930. **$100-125**

**Sterling Tobacco**
Counter display containers filled with 5¢
bags. **$28-40 each**

**Bull Durham Tobacco**
Carton filled with twenty-four bags.
**Carton only $15-25**
**with twenty-four bags $135-150**

**Cardboard Peachey Chewing Tobacco**
**box** **$50-60**

**Sure Shot Chewing Tobacco**
Counter display.                    **$200-300**

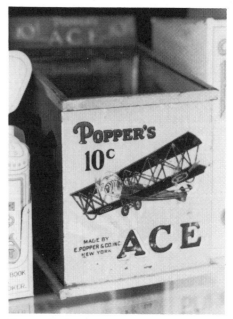

**Popper's Ace**
Counter display for cigars.        **$100-150**

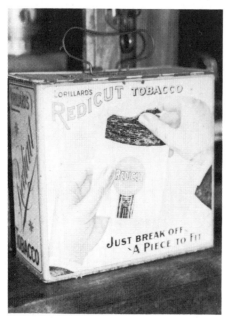

**Redicut Tobacco**
Lunchbox container.                **$55-65**

**Four B.B.B.B. Brand**
Tobacco container                  **$75-85**

**Tiger Chewing Tobacco**
Container originally filled with 5¢
packages. **$125-175**

**Kipling Cut Plug Tobacco**
C. 1910. Box of eight tins **$480-550**
**Each tin $50-60**

**War Eagle Cigar containers**
**$35-55 each**

**Postmaster Cigars**
Counter display. **$100-125**

**Mayo's Cut Plug**
Lunchbox tin                    $95-125

**Two Good Cigars**
Cardboard sign.                 $35-45

**Union Leader Cut Plug**
In "cream can" container.       $55-60

**Bank Note Cigars**
Stand-up counter display.       $100-135

**Collection of lunchbox tins**
C. 1920s. Lunchbox tobacco containers were used by children after the tobacco was removed. They were produced by many tobacco companies from 1910 until the late 1920s.
**$55-65**

**Bull Durham canvas banner**
C. 1920s.

**$75-100**

**Sweet Burley Tobacco**
Counter display with individual packages.
**$115-125**

**Sweet Cuba bucket**
Filled with chewing tobacco. Rare form
with original label. **$200-300**

**Wooden display box**
For a variety of cigarette brands, used on
counter of tobacco shop. **$60-75**

**"Spitting Is Prohibited"**
Sign commonly found in pool halls and
tobacco stores in the 1920s **$30-35**

**Pinch Hit Chewing Tobacco**
Paper banner. $125-175

**Chewing tobacco**
Cylindrical cans, c. 1920. $100-200 each

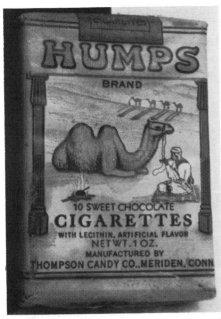

**Humps Chocolate Cigarettes**     $8-12

**Lutz's Frog cigars**     $35-45

**Package of Sweet Caporal cigarettes**
    $5-9

**Fairbanks Fairy Soap**
Decorative interior label.     $125-150

**Box of Lucke's Telescopes cigars**
**$60-80**

**Lucky Strike advertising clock**
"Schoolhouse" form, c. 1915. **$550-650**

**Boxes of Octagon Soap**
Each was delivered filled with one
hundred cakes. **$75-90 each**

**Dake Crackers and Ovens Cakes**
Crackers and biscuit boxes.
**$75-85 each**

**Wall dispenser**
OCB Cigarette Papers.     **$45-55**

**Welcome Soap box**
Colorful label.     **$75-90 each**

**Lautz Brothers soap box**
Factory-dovetailed sides.     **$100-125**

## Ozone Soap and Good Will Soap

Packing boxes, pine, colorful labels. The Good Will Soap box originally was delivered to a grocery store filled with one hundred cakes of soap, weighing seventy-five pounds. The boxes usually were nailed together and decorated with paper or stenciled label. Few of the boxes retained their lids. **$75-95 each**

## Ark Soap box

Paper label. The condition of the label and the amount of color and complexity of the design is critical in determining value. A box without a label has minimal value. **$125-175**

**Lenox Soap box**      **$75-95**

**Soapine box**      **$65-75**

**Acorn Soap box**
Factory-dovetailed sides.          **$75-95**

**Niagara Bakery Crackers and biscuit
box**                              **$75-90**

**Three biscuit boxes**
C. 1910.              **$55-70 each**

**Happy Home Mills coffee bin**
                    **$325-400**

**Sunshine Biscuits**
Displayed with Crescent boxes.
**$55-70 each**

**Red Wolf Coffee tin**          **$28-35**

**Star Mill coffee grinder**
Cast iron, used on the counter in a grocery
store, c. 1900.          **$575-700**

**Red Cough Drops tins**     **$40-50 each**

Bunny Brand coffee can          $35-45

Jam-Boy Coffee can          $30-35

Red Cow Coffee jar          $95-115

Red Cow Coffee tin          $150-165

Dining Car Coffee tin       $28-35

Wooden coffee box       $100-135

Bob White Table Syrup can    $20-25

**Schlosser's Ice Cream sign**
C. 1940.       $45-55

**Uncle John's Syrup**
Stand-up or counter display.    $125-150

**Ferndell Coffee tins**
larger tin $30-35
smaller tin $28-32

**Fresh Roasted Coffee**
Montgomery Ward & Company, c. 1920.
smaller tin $40-45
larger tin $60-75

**Mid-nineteenth century lantern**
Adapted to be used in a late-nineteenth
to early-twentieth century country store.
"Ice Cream and Pop" painted on lantern.
Found in Ohio.                    **$200-250**

**Display milk bottles**
Union Grove Milk, c. 1920.                    **$20-25 each**

**Log Cabin Tin**             **$75-100**

**Frontier Inn Log Cabin tin**   **$200-235**

**Towle's Log Cabin Syrup**
"Stand-up" for counter display. Heavy cardboard.

                                              **$500-750**

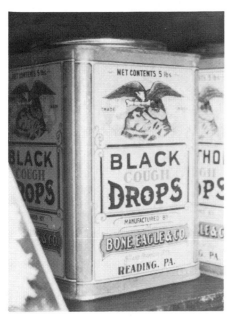

Black Cough Drops tin          $30-35

Mr. Peanut jar          $150-175

DeLaval Cream Separator parts box
C. 1915.          $500-575

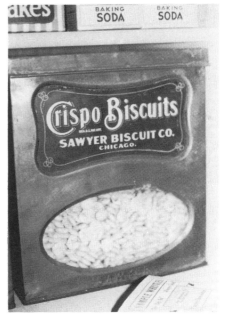

Crispo Biscuits
Counter container.          $50-55

**Variety of paper bags**
For ground coffee.                  **$3-4 each**

**Round Coca-Cola sign**
From the late 1940s.                **$45-55**

**Carnation Malted Milk container**
                                    **$8-12**

**Coca-Cola display cart**
C. 1950.                            **$75-100**

Left: Cast iron string holder · $500-600

Below: Frog mechanical bank $600-750

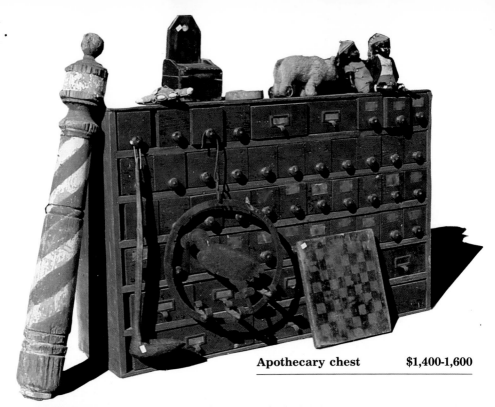

**Apothecary chest**      **$1,400-1,600**

**Bunny Brand Rolled Oats container**
**$85-100**

**Jersey Coffee bin**      **$400-475**

Left: Seal of North Carolina
stand-up                    $75-95

Below: Sweet Cuba Tobacco
containers        $125-150 each

**Painted basket** $200-250

**Painted storage basket**     **$600-800**

**Splint utility baskets**     **$75-100 each**

**Oak seed boxes** $75-85

**Hiram Sibley seed box** $375-400

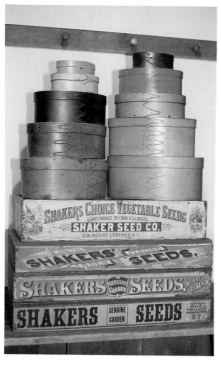

**Above: Northrup King seed display**
**$150-175**

**Top left: Firkin and butter boxes**
**$300-500 each**

**Bottom left: Shaker oval boxes and**
**seed boxes**

175

**Tuf Mut display overalls** $125-150

**Beech-Nut counter display**
Period packages of chewing gum.
**for display $275-325**
**per pack of gum $15-25**

**Metal fire bucket**
Designed to be hung in meeting or lodge
hall. Probably repainted and stenciled.
**$25-35**

**National Biscuit Company**
Counter container. **$50-55**

**Johnston counter container**
For cookies. **$50-55**

**Metal containers for Yucatan Gum**
**$55-65 each**

**Heide's Diamond Licorice**
Gum drops box. **$12-15**

**Wrigley's counter display** **$50-60**

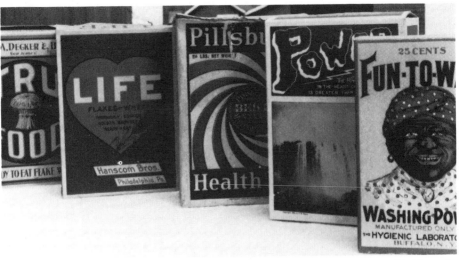

**Cereal and washing powder boxes** **$8-20 each**

**Miller-Parrott Baking Company**
Counter container.                    **$50-55**

**Quality Biscuit Company**
Counter container.                    **$50-55**

**Coca-Cola metal sign**      **$25-30**

**Power Cereal box**      **$8-10**

**Pillsbury's Health Bran box**     **$8-9**

**Life Flakes of Wheat box**     **$8-9**

**Tru Food cereal box**     **$10-12**

**B-B-B-B Rolled Oats**     **$14-16 each**

**Handy Candy dispenser**
For 5¢ bars, c. 1950.                    **$50-65**

**White Villa**
Pure Spices container.                    **$6-8**

**Hales Midget Pop Corn box**
                              **$8-10 each**

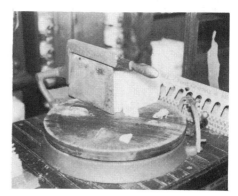

**Grocery store**
Cheese slicer.                    **$150-175**

**Partridge Pure Lard tin**  $12-14

**Mother's Crushed Oats**  $14-16

**Smith Brothers Cough Drops**
Counter display.  $75-95

**J. Monroe Taylor's Soda**
Paper and wood.  $45-55

**Elliott's Juvenile Shoes**
Premium used by children to roll barrel hoops, c. 1910.  $28-35

**Re-Joyce Rolled Oats**
Cylindrical container.                    **$14-16**

**Wolff Milling Company**
Flour barrel.                             **$130-150**

**Jell-o box**
C. 1925.                                  **$3-5**

**Boot display**
Oversized, c. 1950                        **$55-65**

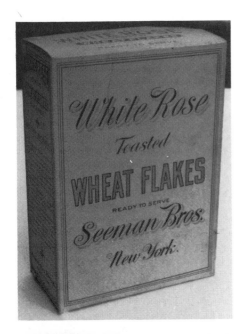

**Blue Bell Rolled Oats**        **$12-14**

**White Rose Toasted Wheat Flakes**
C. 1930.        **$8-10**

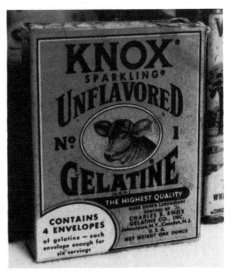

**Knox Gelatine box**        **$2-4**

King Syrup tins        **$20-24 each**

**J. & P. Coats' spool cabinet**
C. 1900.  If old and original: **$200-225**

**Atwood Suspender advertising sign**
On heavy cardboard, c. 1890.  **$500-600**

**Spool cabinet**
From a distance, the J. & P. Coats' spool cabinet looked to be original.  With a closer look, it is obvious that it had been relettered with a brush, thus worth only **$50-75**.

**Our Mother's Cocoa tins**
larger tin **$24-28**
smaller tin **$18-24**

**Shaker Garden Seed boxes**
Mt. Lebanon, New York. Late nineteenth century. **$550-650 each**

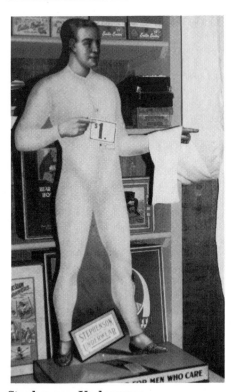

**Stephenson Underwear**
Stand-up for displaying underwear, c. 1915. **$3,000-4,500**

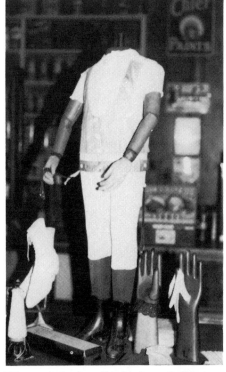

**Mannequin for displaying clothing**
Without head **$125-200**
With head **$275-350**

The "Ideal" clip-on tie      $8-10

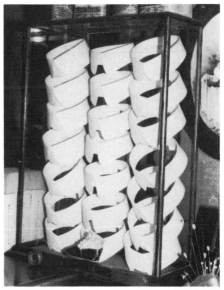

Oak collar display case      $200-275

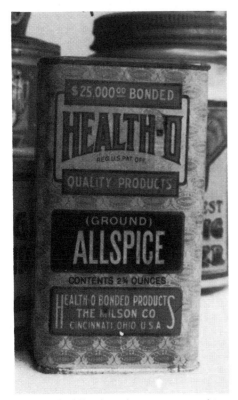

Health-O Allspice tin      $3-5

Stay Prest Trouser Presser      $20-25

**Advertising match holder**
From the Brown Shoe Company, c. 1880.
**$400-600**

**Tuf Mut overalls**
Denim, oversized for display, almost 11'
from top to bottom, found in Nebraska, c.
1930. **$125-150**

**Borax**
Paper advertising sign.  **$100-125**

**Old Dutch Cleanser**
Floor display stand-up.  **$100-125**

**Seed chest**  **$225-250**

**Magic Washer Soap**  **$6-9**

**Individual packets or seed "papers"**      **$1-2 each**

**Oak shelving**
From a central Illinois drugstore, c. 1900.
**$800-1,200**

**Humphreys' Specifics storage cabinet**
For nonprescription "cure-alls." Oak cabinet, c. 1910.      **$400-575**

**Savoy Toilet Paper**
C. 1900.      per package **$20-25**

**Onion Skin toilet tissue**
C. 1900.      per roll **$15-20**

**Cans of Gold Dust**
Scouring Cleanser.              **$14-18 each**

**Ex-Lax stand-up**
From the 1920s.                **$150-225**

**Fun-To-Wash Washing Powder box**
                               **$24-28**

**Blabon display board**
For linoleum.                  **$50-70**

**Browns Seed display case**
C. 1920.                    $225-275

**Washing machine**
C. 1910.                    $150-175

**Diamond Dye cabinet**      $65-75

**Bartlett's Blue Ball box**    $55-65

**Broom holder**
Merkle's Blu-J Brooms, c. 1920.
**$150-175**

**Fire extinguishers**
Filled with chemicals, c. 1915.
**$35-45 each**

**Putnam metal dye cabinet**
C. 1940s. **$75-100**

**Packages of Elephant Steel Wool**
**$8-10 each**

**Fibre Brooms**
Wire holder for brooms, c. 1930. **$55-65**

**Chickencock Whiskey tin**
Empty. **$25-30**

**Silk Tissue**
C. 1900. per roll **$8-10**

**Putnam metal dye cabinet**
C. 1935 **$50-60**

**Oak counter**
With storage and display area, c. 1900.

**$800-$1,000**

**Glass storage bottles**
Commonly used in drugstores in early 1900s.

**$65-75 each**

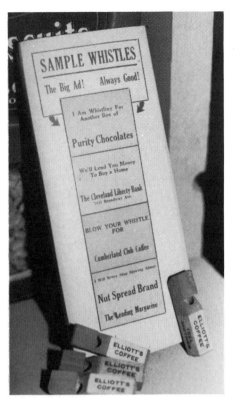

**Box of sample whistles**
From Elliott's Coffee. If your name is Elliott, the whistles are worth considerably more than $20-28 dollars. **$20-28**

**Dy-o-la Dyes metal cabinet**
C. 1930s. **$100-125**

Interior of Dy-o-la cabinet.

Original boxes of Dy-o-la dyes in cabinet.

**Kerosene lanterns**
C. 1930.

$35-50 each

**Cole's "Hot Blast" Stove**
Canvas sign.

$100-115

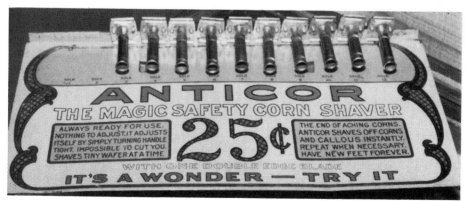

**Anticor corn shavers and stand-up**

$75-100

Wildroot metal sign          $45-55

**Entrance sign**
Metal, hand painted, c. 1890.          **$55-75**

**United States Express**
Money order sign.          **$125-150**

**Collins Safety Razor stand-up**
          **$150-225**

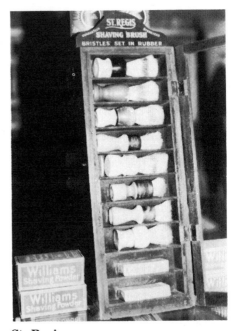

**St. Regis**
Shaving brush display case          **$75-100**

**Bull Dog Jar Rubbers**
Stand-up counter display and original boxes.

for stand-up **$20-25**
for each box **$2-3**

**One-cent scales**
C. 1930.

In working order **$225-275 each**

**Chicago American newspaper box**
For selling the evening edition.**$150-175**

**Gasoline sign**
C. 1950.                                    **$65-75**

# 6 Potpourri

**Black doll**
Late nineteenth to early twentieth century.     **$300-375**

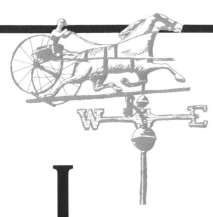

In other sections of this book, we have pictured and priced decorated stoneware, furniture, baskets, country store antiques, and a wide variety of kitchen and hearth antiques.

We have included a potpourri section in each of the previous five editions of this book to cover the numerous categories that do not fall within one of the preceding chapters.

**Round the World with Nellie Bly**      **$110-125**

**Cast iron frogs**
Given away with the purchase of a windmill and counter-balance weight, c. 1900.
**$45-75 each**

**Unpainted short-stemmed rooster**
On a ball-shaped base, Elgin, Illinois, c. 1900. **$500-600**

**Short-stemmed rooster**
Made by the Elgin Wind Power and Pump Company of Elgin, Illinois, c. 1900. The rooster is resting on the upper half of a ball-shaped base that could be filled with rocks or small pieces of metal for additional weight. **$450-550**

**"Hanchett" bull**
With replaced horns, painted, c. early 1900s. **$675-800**

**"Woodmanse" rooster**
Probably made by the Elgin Wind Power and Pump Company, c. 1900. **$600-700**

**Larger Elgin rooster**
In original paint, c. 1900.                                    $700-800
**Crescent-moon-shaped governor weight**
Marked "Eclipse," made by Fairbanks, Morse and Company of Chicago, Illinois. This eclipse is called a "wet" moon because it was hung with its points up to catch the rain.
$100-125

**Fairbury bull**
Made by the Fairbury (Nebraska) Windmill Company, 1910–1920. There are four variations of the flat Fairbury bulls. The two bulls illustrated here do not have their original bases.          **$500-600**

**Short-tail or bobtail horse**
Demptster Mill Manufacturing Company of Beatrice, Nebraska, c. 1910–1930.
$150-225

The tail on this Fairbury bull is separated from the body of the bull. Seldom is the bull found with an unbroken tail.

**Long-tail horse**
Dempster Mill Manufacturing Company,
c. early 1900s. **$300-400**

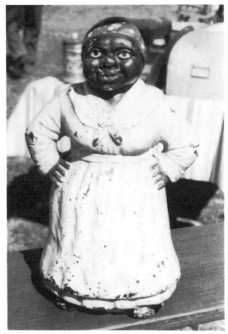

**Cast iron door stop**
C. 1915, original paint. If this door stop
had been repainted, it would have lost
much of its value, regardless of its age.
**$150-175**

**Squirrel weight**
Elgin Wind Power and Pump Company, c.
early 1900s. **$1,200-1,600**

**Whirligig**
Found in Nebraska, c. 1915. **$150-225**

**Buggy wheel**
Early twentieth century.　**$25-30 each**

**Wagon wheels**
Early twentieth century.　**$40-45 each**

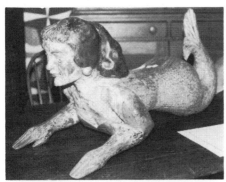

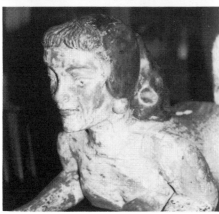

**Mermaid carving**
C. early twentieth century.　**$650-725**

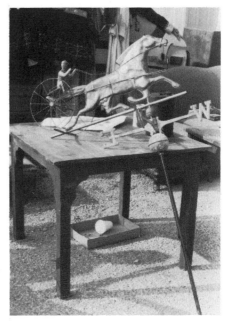

**Reproduction weathervane**
Copper with directionals.  If it's old, it's worth a minimum of $3,000.　**$125-175**

**Horse weathervane**
C. 1915.                    **$150-175**

**Baseball clock**
C. 1940.                    **$45-55**

**Painted birdhouse**
Twentieth century. Birdhouses are almost
impossible to date. The exposure to several years' winters can age them quickly.
                           **$8-12**

**Factory-made wall clocks**
Early 1900s, factory-made of oak.
                    **$150-250 each**

**Regulator wall clock**
Oak, original varnished finish, c. 1900.
$225-275

**Tin cylindrical candle box**
Designed to be hung. Original paint, c. 1850.
$225-300

**Candle box**
Dovetailed sides, orange "wash" finish, New England, c. 1840. A wash is made by diluting paint to the point that, when it is applied to wood, the grain still shows.
$400-485

**Saucer-based brass candlesticks**
English, mid-nineteenth century. $125-150 each

**Hog scraper candlestick**
Unusually long shaft, c. 1840. **$250-275**

**Painted tin spice chest**
Factory made, c. 1880, stenciled lettering.
**$200-250**

**Assortment of graniteware kitchen utensils**
C. 1920. **$35-75 each piece**

**Spice chest**
Original porcelain knobs, c. 1900, factory-made.                          **$135-150**

**Pine wagon seats**
From farm wagons, c. early twentieth century, painted.            **$85-120 each**

**Enterprise fruit press**
Stenciled decoration, cast iron, c. 1900, mass-produced.                 **$100-125**

**Cast iron pump**                          **$55-75**

**Tin "kitchen" or metal storage piece**
C. late nineteenth century, replaced porcelain knobs, painted finish. Tin "kitchens" contained storage areas for coffee, sugar, flour, and a variety of spices. Many came equipped with flour sifters or coffee grinders mounted on sides.    **$375-475**

**Oak treadle-based sewing table**
With Damascus sewing machine, c. 1915.
                    **$150-175**

**Coffee mill or grinder**
Original stenciled front, replaced porcelain knob, c. 1900, factory produced.
                    **$75-85**

**Oak telephone**
C. 1920s, commonly used in rural areas into the 1960s.
        in working order **$150-200**

**Cast iron kettle**
Goose neck and bail handle, 1900.
$35-45

**Silhouette geese decoys**
Original painted finish, c. 1930.
**$75-85 each**

**Cast iron crossing signs**
C. 1950. **$15-18 each** section

**Collection of axes**
Maple handles. **$35-45 each**

**Wooden wringers**
C. early twentieth century.                          **$20-35 each**

**"Perfect Washer"**
Painted pine with original stenciled decoration, patent date of 1889.    **$185-225**

**Bentwood butter churn**
Factory made, c. 1900.          **$100-125**

**Factory-made butter churn**
C. early 1900s.              **$125-140 each**

**"Number 1 Small Family Size" butter
churn**
Factory made, c. 1900.          **$100-150**

**Barrel butter churn**
Staved construction with metal handles,
painted finish, c. 1870.          **$200-250**

**Dasher butter churn**
Painted finish, staved construction with
metal bands, c. 1870.          **$250-300**

**Dish-drying rack**
"Pin" construction, original finish, c. 1860. **$325-350**

**Sugar buckets or firkins**
Pine, staved construction, wooden bands, bail or "drop" handles, c. late nineteenth to early twentieth century, painted finishes. **$150-175 each**

**Shaker oval tub**
Pine, staved construction with lappers or fingers, c. mid-nineteenth century, New England, painted. **$675-825**

**Sugar buckets**
Wooden drop handles. Painted, staved construction, late nineteenth to early twentieth century. **$150-175**

214

**Shaker carrier**
Hickory handle with a pine bottom and maple sides, New England, c. late nineteenth century.  **$850-1,200**

**Shaker cheese boxes**
"Button" or interlocking hoops, New England, painted finishes, nineteenth century.  **$450-650 each**

**Stack of Shaker boxes**
Oval, pine top and bottom with maple sides, New England, nineteenth century.  **$650-2,000 each**

**Hooked rug**
C. 1900.                                                                    **$150-225**

**Carved pine horse**
Without its original rockers. Worn paint,
late nineteenth century.        **$325-385**

**Rag rugs**
First half of the twentieth century.
**$75-150 each**

**Rocking horse**
Carved pine, repainted, late nineteenth century. **$625-700**

**"Homemade" rocking horse**
Pine, twentieth century. **$150-175**

**Rocking horse**
Hide-covered pine, original tack, late nineteenth century.  This horse did double-duty.
It could be removed from the rockers and pushed across the room on its wheeled plat-
form.                                                                                         **$750-1,000**

**Child's "Express" wagon**
On iron wheels, stenciled, replaced wooden handle, 1890–1910.                **$225-275**

**Dollhouse**
First half of the twentieth century.
**$50-65**

**Dollhouse**
"Homemade," twentieth century.
**$50-65**

**Pine carpenter's chest**
With iron handles, early twentieth century.
**$135-165**

**Carved jointed doll**
Pine, early twentieth century, 10″ tall.
**$95-115**

**Black doll**
C. 1930.
**$95-135**

**Black dolls**
C. 1940. $55-75 each

**Steiff bear**
"Loved" condition, c. 1915. **$300-375**

**Steiff bear**
C. 1940s. **$225-250**

**Dollhouse**
C. 1930, commercially made. **$75-85**

**Cloth dolls**
Early 1900s. **$100-175 each**

**Painted carving**
Wagon, team, and husband and wife on a walnut base, early 1900s. **$500-625**

**Carved clown**
From a larger grouping of circus animals and performers, probably made in Germany, c. 1910. **$115-125**

**Stuffed animals on wheels**
Designed to be ridden by an infant, c. 1940 **$75-90**

We have watched in recent years as the prices of baskets, birdhouses, teddy bears, granite ware, and windmill weights have steadily risen. Children's board games and puzzles in their original boxes will soon be joining the list. The games, puzzles, and books that follow all date from the 1880–1915 period and are complete, without any missing parts.

Locomotive Picture Puzzle     $75-100

Fine Table Croquet     $50-65

The New Bicycle Game     $75-100

Boy's Own Football Game     $150-200

The Rough Riders     $125-175

The Fast Mail     $175-200

The Popular Game of Golf     $50-75

Round the World
with Nellie Bly                    $110-125

Advance and Retreat          $75-90

Game of Catching Mice        $100-125

Game of the Water Melon Patch
                    $150-225

The Darktown Brigade
Fire Picture Puzzle          $135-150

The Engine Picture Puzzle    $75-100

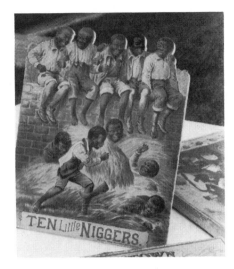

Ten Little Niggers    $100-150

The Game of Golf    $100-125

Wild West Picture Puzzle    $65-75

The tin wind-up toys that follow were made in the 1930s and early 1940s. The toys illustrated here are all in working order, and several have their original cardboard containers.

Four-passenger open roadster $55-75

Amos 'N' Andy open car    $300-350

**Checker Taxi Cab**      **$100-125**

**Motorcycle**      **$75-100**

**Touring car**      **$75-100**

**Roadster**      **$75-100**

**Joe Penner**
**"Wanna' buy a duck?"**      **$250-275**

**Black man with a chicken    $650-750**

**Unique Artie clown and car $100-125**

**Ferris Wheel                                      $55-75**

**Charleston Trio** $200-250

**Spark Plug and Barney toy** $800-900

**Toonerville Trolley** $300-425

**Cabin bank** $55-65

**Barney Google
and Spark Plug Game** $100-125

**Flapping Beetle** $45-55

**Uncle Wiggley car** $50-65

**Contemporary folk art carving**
$400-475

**Collection of purses**                                    **$25-50 each**

**Children's hats**
C. 1910.                                                    **$25-35 each**

**Metal truck**
C. 1940.                    **$75-90**

**Handmade farm wagon**
Twentieth century.          **$150-175**

**Baby carriage**
Made of wicker, c. 1920.  **$100-125**

Gambling wheel  **$100-135**

**Child's wagon**
With wooden wheels, c. 1920.  **$100-125**

**Plastic Christmas ornament.**
C. 1920.  **$25-30 pair**

**Feather trees**
Made in Germany, c. 1920.
> Larger tree and base **$225-250**
> Smaller tree and base **$175-200**

**George L. Edinger's sled**
C. 1910. **$150-220**

**Child's wagon**
C. 1920. **$95-125**

**Checkerboard**
Early twentieth century. **$150-225**

# Final
# Examination

We have contacted several major universities to see if they would assist us in administering this test. To certify the scores, we wanted all participants to complete the exercise within a university setting. To date we have had no response from any of the institutions. Recently we received a positive response from a franchised taxidermy school in Idaho.

Until we establish a formal relationship with the school, we will use the same procedures that have successfully

failed most of those who have taken final examinations in earlier editions of this book.

You will be receiving a postcard soon explaining travel arrangements for the next examination. If you fail this exam, please destroy the card when you receive it. Be advised that we will be cross-checking. If you pass the test, please return the card to your local Ma's Midget Grocery.

## Directions

1. Read each question carefully. If you need help, consult your local librarian.
2. Don't write on your neighbor's coat.
3. Don't take the exam in the back of a moving truck or near an open flame.
4. Remove any sharp articles from the room before you score the test.
5. Your final score will be verified and sent to your homeroom teacher and your aunt. If you do not have an aunt, one will be provided.

1. This piece of furniture dates from about
   a. 1790–1820
   b. 1845–1865
   c. after 1875

2. It was used primarily
   a. in the bedroom
   b. in the kitchen
   c. on the porch

3. Its primary function was to _____ .

4. If you were to describe it, you would call it a _____ .

5. (True) (False) The piece was factory-made.

6. (True) (False) It is probably made of pine.

7. Its approximate value is
   a. $75-100
   b. $175-250
   c. $375-500
   d. more than $500

8. (True) (False) This could be called an example of "country" furniture.

9. (True) (False) This piece is made of stoneware rather than redware.

10. This example could best be described as a
    a. jug
    b. jar
    c. crock
    d. none of the above

11. The "5" was put on the piece with a
    a. stencil
    b. slip cup
    c. brush
    d. none of the above

12. The Red Wing Pottery was located in
    a. New York
    b. Pennsylvania
    c. Illinois
    d. none of the above

13. (True) (False) Abraham Lincoln could have purchased this piece to store his potatoes.

14. (True) (False) This is a "Boston" rocking chair.

15. The arms of many rocking chairs of this type were unpainted and made of
    a. pine
    b. cherry
    c. oak
    d. walnut

16. (True) (False) This chair does *not* have a crest rail.

17. The seats of similar rocking chairs were usually made of
    a. pine
    b. cherry
    c. oak
    d. walnut

18. What is the approximate value of this chair?
    a. $100-175
    b. $225-275
    c. more than $300 but less than $500
    d. more than $500

19. This mixing bowl dates from about
    a. 1820–1840
    b. 1850–1870
    c. 1880–1910
    d. after 1930

20. The decoration on the bowl was applied with a
    a. brush
    b. sponge
    c. stencil
    d. none of the above

21. (True) (False) Stoneware mixing bowls usually carry a maker's mark to identify the pottery in which they were made.

22. (True) (False) This bowl was molded rather than hand "thrown" on a potter's wheel.

23. In which states are most pie safes found?
    a. Vermont, Maine, New Hampshire
    b. South Dakota, Nebraska, North Dakota
    c. Texas, New Mexico, Arizona
    d. Indiana, Illinois, Ohio

24. This painted pie safe is probably made of
    a. pine
    b. cherry
    c. oak
    d. walnut

25. Which color would add the most value to the pie safe?
    a. red
    b. green
    c. white
    d. blue

26. What is the approximate value of this safe?
    a. $100-200
    b. $300-500
    c. more than $500

27. (True) (False) This country rocking chair was factory-made in the mid-nineteenth century.

28. Ths seat of this chair is made of
    a. oak splint
    b. cane
    c. rattan
    d. "Shaker" woolen tapes

29. This chair could best be described as a
    a. bannister-back
    b. ladder-back
    c. step-back
    d. none of the above

30. (True) (False) Most rocking chairs were made almost entirely of pine.

31. This is a stoneware _____
_____

32. The decoration was put on with a
   a. stencil
   b. slip cup
   c. brush
   d. none of the above

33. (True) (False) This example was hand thrown.

34. What is the approximate value of this piece?
   a. $100-175
   b. $200-275
   c. $300-375
   d. more than $450

35. This dry sink dates from about
   a. 1820
   b. 1840
   c. 1860
   d. after 1880

36. (True) (False) The front of this dry sink could be described as wainscoted.

37. (True) (False) If you had an opportunity to purchase this dry sink in white paint for $505, it would be a good buy.

38. A more scholarly name for a sugar bucket is _____ .

39. (True) (False) This example dates from before 1800.

40. (True) (False) "Buttonhole" hoops are found on most sugar buckets.

41. The approximate value of this red-painted sugar bucket is
   a. $75-125
   b. $150-175
   c. $225-300
   d. more than $400

42. Butter stamps can be handcarved or machine stamped. This one is

_____ _____ .

43. Which one of the designs listed below would be the rarest on a butter stamp?
   a. rose
   b. tulip
   c. strawbrry and vine
   d. cow and a calf

44. (True) (False) This butter stamp is worth at least $175.

45. Which of the two baskets is the most desirable?
   a. the one on the left
   b. the one on the right
   c. they are of equal value

46. Most country baskets are made of _____ or _____ splint.
   a. walnut
   b. ash
   c. pine
   d. oak
   e. a and c are both correct
   f. b and c are both correct
   g. b and d are both correct

Match the following antiques authorities with their areas of specialization.

47. _____ Doug Hamel

48. _____ William Grande

49. _____ Alan Weintraub

50. _____ M.E. Gould
   a. decorated stoneware
   b. woodenware and tinware
   c. stonewall construction
   d. Shaker
   e. hooked rugs

**Bonus** (worth five points)

What is the approximate value of this man?

  a. $50-75
  b. $100-175
  c. $275
  d. more than $1,000

**Answers**

1. c; 2. a; 3. store a chamber pot; 4. commode; 5. true; 6. false; 7. b; 8. false; 9. true; 10. crock; 11. a; 12. d; 13. false; 14. false—Salem rocking chair; 15. b; 16. false; 17. a; 18. c; 19. c; 20. b; 21. false; 22. true; 23. d; 24. a; 25. d; 26. c; 27. false; 28. a; 29. b; 30. false; 31. milk pan; 32. brush; 33. true; 34. c; 35. d; 36. true; 37. false; 38. firken; 39. false; 40. false; 41. c; 42. hand carved; 43. d; 44. true; 45. b; 46. g; 47. d; 48. a; 49. c; 50. b; Bonus question c.

## Scoring

Number Correct

| | |
|---|---|
| 46–50 | You have been nominated as a board member of historical societies in Dupo, Illinois, and Argyle, Texas. Their directors will be in contact with you. Wait by your telephone. They will only call once. |
| 41–45 | A short man with a long stick will soon be stopping by to beat your rugs. There will be no charge for his services, but he may want a sandwich. |
| 36–40 | Your name will be sent to every antiques dealer in the United States. You will be forced to pay retail. |
| 31–35 | Forget the trip to Idaho. Your picture will be prominently displayed in the thousands of Ma's Midget Grocery stores across America. |
| 30 or less | Put all sharp articles *back* in the room and run the hot water. |

# About the Authors

**D**on and Carol Raycraft, authors of twenty-six books on country antiques, live with their three sons on a four generation farm near Normal, Illinois. They reside in a mid-nineteenth century barn that has been charmingly decorated and furnished in Shaker and American country antiques by Carol, a nationally known interior designer. Both attended Illinois State University where she received a bachelor's degree in elementary education and her husband earned a bachelor's, master's, and doctoral degree in education and psychology.